EXPLORING THE SNOW ROADS

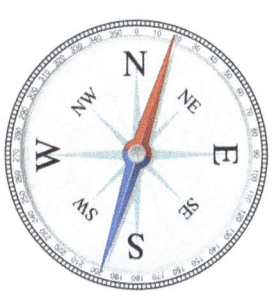

David M. Addison

Other Books by David M. Addison

A Meander in Menorca
Bananas about La Palma
Misadventures in Tuscany
An Innocent Abroad
Confessions of a Banffshire Loon
The Cuban Missus Crisis
Still Innocent Abroad
Exploring the NC500
Travels Through Time in Italy
Travels Around Sorrento
Exploring the SWC300

EXPLORING THE SNOW ROADS

A Cultural and Historical Companion to the Snow Roads Scenic Route

David M. Addison

Exploring the Snow Roads: A Cultural and Historical Companion to the Snow Roads Scenic Route by David M. Addison

First edition published in Great Britain in 2020 by Extremis Publishing Ltd., Suite 218, Castle House, 1 Baker Street, Stirling, FK8 1AL, United Kingdom.
www.extremispublishing.com

Extremis Publishing is a Private Limited Company registered in Scotland (SC509983) whose Registered Office is Suite 218, Castle House, 1 Baker Street, Stirling, FK8 1AL, United Kingdom.

Copyright © David M. Addison, 2020.

David M. Addison has asserted the moral right under the Copyright, Designs and Patents Act 1988 to be identified as the author of this work.

The views expressed in this work are solely those of the author, and do not necessarily reflect those of the publisher. The publisher hereby disclaims any responsibility for them.

This book is a work of non-fiction. Unless otherwise noted, the author and the publisher make no explicit guarantees as to the accuracy of the information included in this book and, in some cases, the names of people, places and organisations have been altered to protect their privacy.

This book may include references to organisations, feature films, television programmes, popular songs, musical bands, novels, reference books, and other creative works, the titles of which are trademarks and/or registered trademarks, and which are the intellectual properties of their respective copyright holders.

All rights reserved. No part of this publication may be reproduced, stored in a retrieval system, or transmitted, in any form or by any means, electronic, mechanical, photocopying, recording or otherwise, without the prior permission in writing of the publisher.

This book is sold subject to the condition that it shall not, by way of trade or otherwise, be lent, re-sold or hired out, or otherwise circulated without the publisher's prior consent in any form of binding or cover other than that in which it is published and without a similar condition including this condition being imposed on the subsequent purchaser.

A CIP catalogue record for this book is available from the British Library.

ISBN: 978-1-9996962-3-8

Typeset in Goudy Bookletter 1911, designed by The League of Moveable Type.
Printed and bound in Great Britain by IngramSpark, Chapter House, Pitfield, Kiln Farm, Milton Keynes, MK11 3LW, United Kingdom.

Cover artwork is Copyright © AlexanderM UK at Shutterstock Inc.
Cover design and book design is Copyright © Thomas A. Christie.
Incidental vector artwork from Pixabay.

Author image and internal photographic images are Copyright © David M. Addison and Fiona J. Addison and are sourced from their private collection, unless otherwise stated.

The copyrights of third parties are reserved. All third party imagery is used under the provision of Fair Use for the purposes of commentary and criticism.

While every reasonable effort has been made to contact copyright holders and secure permission for all images reproduced in this work, we offer apologies for any instances in which this was not possible and for any inadvertent omissions.

For Fiona

Facilitator and Photographer

Map of the Snow Roads Scenic Route
and its surroundings

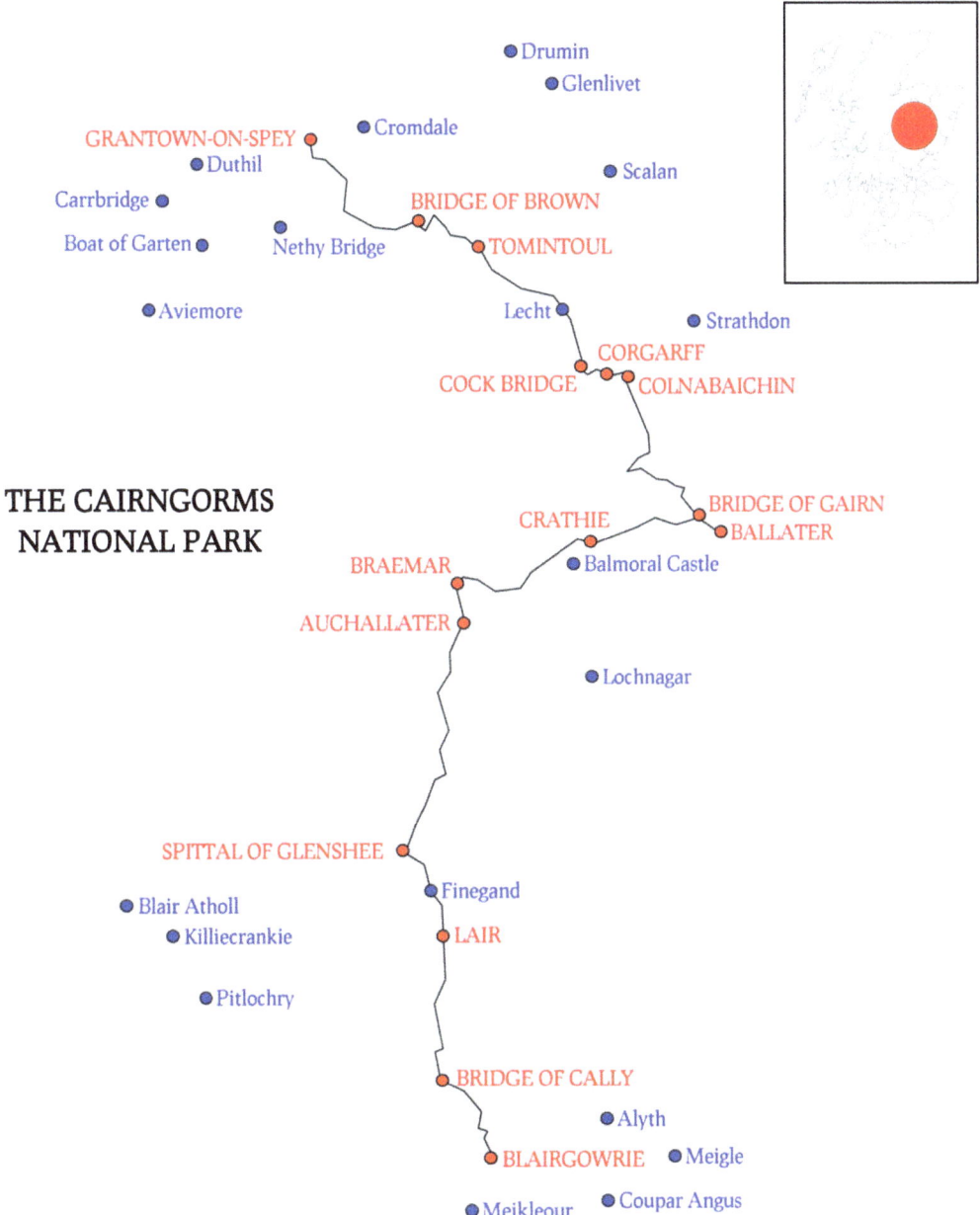

Contents

1. **Meikleour**: The Hedge and the House ... Page 1
2. **Blairgowrie and Rattray**: Faith and Fruit ... Page 9
3. **West of Blairgowrie**: A Fake, a Ghost and a Polymath ... Page 15
4. **Alyth**: The Arches, the Instrument Maker and the Drunks' Cart ... Page 21
5. **Meigle and Coupar Angus**: Stories in Stones ... Page 29
6. **Blairgowrie to Finegand**: A Tale of a Cockerell ... Page 39
7. **Finegand to the Glenshee Ski Centre**: A "Grave" and the Devil's Elbow ... Page 45
8. **Braemar**: A Castle, a Saint, a Teller of Tales and Two Memorials ... Page 53
9. **Braemar**: Games, Gatherings, a Lodge and a Gorge ... Page 61
10. **Braemar Castle**: Bobbing John, the Black Colonel and *La Belle Rebelle* ... Page 69
11. **Balmoral and Lochnagar**: Much Ado about Royalty ... Page 79
12. **Abergeldie and Birkhall**: A Tale of Two Castles ... Page 89
13. **Ballater**: The Station and the Shops ... Page 93
14. **Beyond Ballater**: Wonderful Water, Knights Templar and Knights of the Road ... Page 99
15. **Corgarff**: A Very Unlucky Castle ... Page 109
16. **Over the Lecht**: The Postmistress, the Ski Centre and the Well ... Page 115
17. **Tomintoul**: The Laird, the Swindler and the Mutineer ... Page 121
18. **Glenlivet**: Two Distilleries and a Seminary ... Page 129
19. **Glenlivet**: Castles and Battles ... Page 137
20. **Grantown-on-Spey**: The Very Model of a Modern Town and a Castle ... Page 145
21. **Grantown-on-Spey**: Trains and Toilets ... Page 153
22. **Huntly's Cave and Duthil**: A Hidey-Hole and a Cemetery ... Page 159
23. **Carrbridge and Boat of Garten**: A Bridge and a Bird ... Page 165

Image Credits ... Page 171
About the Author ... Page 173

Acknowledgements

For their assistance and information imparted, my grateful thanks to, as I encountered them:

- **Donald Livingstone** of Alyth Museum

- **Andrew MacThomas** of Finegand, 19th Chief of Clan MacThomas

- **Jonathan Findlay**, President, Clan Farquharson UK

- **Martin Simpson** of the Deeside Water Company, Pannanich

- **Andrew Campbell** of Ballater Tourist Information Centre

- **Aileen Lawrence** and **Carol the Cook** of the Glenshee Snow Sports Centre

- **Steve Calvert** of the Tomintoul and Glenlivet Discovery Centre

EXPLORING THE SNOW ROADS

A Cultural and Historical Companion to the Snow Roads Scenic Route

Chapter One

Meikleour: The Hedge and the House

ANYONE who is coming north on the A93 from Perth to Blairgowrie in order to start exploring the Snow Roads Scenic Route will find, just four miles before the town, a very impressive sight. It is the Meikleour Beech Hedge, one-third of a mile long and one hundred feet high, and which – since 1996 – has been officially regarded as the longest and the highest hedge in Britain. Don't take my word for it – the *Guinness Book of Records* said so, and the editors are rigorous in the checking of facts.

It was planted in 1745 by Robert Murray Nairne and his wife Jean Mercer, daughter of Sir Laurence Mercer and heiress of the estates of Aldie near Perth. They married in 1720 but I am sorry to tell you they did not live happily ever after in the grand house they built at Meikelour. They were Jacobite supporters and Robert left to do his duty for the cause along with the men who actually did the planting of the hedge.

The laird and the planters never came back, their lives cut short in that conflict which, as everyone knows, ended in inglorious defeat at Culloden on 16th April 1746. The hedge, however, was allowed to grow higher and higher in their memory. It also served to screen the house from the road. The grief-stricken widow left Meikleour, never to return. Instead, she hied herself to Edinburgh where she kept a low profile amongst the much more numerous citizens of the capital. She died there on 1st December 1749.

Being of beech (*Fagus sylvatica*) it is a hedge for all seasons, arguably at its finest in the autumn when it exchanges its spring and summer leaves of lush green for those of russet and gold. It is a sight to be seen at any time of year and you should, if you can. After twenty years during which it was allowed to grow unruly, it was given a much-needed trim in November 2019 after Perth and Kinross Council finally came to an agreement with the owners, Sam Mercer Nairne and his French wife, Claire, who were facing a massive bill of £90,000 to maintain this world-champion hedge.

It used to be kept nice and trim by four men from the estate. Standing on top of a hydraulic lift and armed with hedge trimmers, it once took them six weeks to complete the task. Now, in these health-and-safety conscious times (not to say litigious), the traffic must be managed which meant closing the stretch of road completely. An inconvenience to be sure, but at least it was all over in six days – like ripping off an Elastoplast all at once instead of hair by painful hair.

Meikleour Beech Hedge, before it was trimmed

The house that the hedge conceals was redesigned in 1870 in the style of a French chateau by the renowned Scottish architect, David Bryce (1803-1876), who – amongst his other list of credits – can lay claim to many of Edinburgh's most notable buildings such as the Bank of Scotland Headquarters on the Mound. I pick that out for special mention simply because anyone who has ever been to Edinburgh must have seen it, either from below on Princes Street, or down the Mound from the Royal Mile.

Bryce was given the commission for the house by Emily Jane Mercer Elphinstone de Flahault (1819-95), and if you think that sounds a trifle French you would be right. Her father was Auguste Charles Joseph de Flahault, Compte de Flahault de la Billardrie (1785-1870). He was one of Napoleon's star generals and fought with distinction in the disastrous Russian campaign of 1812. He was rewarded by being created Brigadier General and aide-de-camp to Napoleon the following year. He served him well until the even more disastrous Battle of Waterloo – from the French point of view, of course.

In June 1817, the Compte (who was not short of offers from the ladies), settled down and married Margaret Mercer Elphinstone (1788-1867) in Edinburgh. She was the only child of Admiral, 1st Viscount Keith, aka Sir George Keith Elphinstone (1746-1823), and Jean Mercer, daughter of Colonel William Mercer of Aldie, Perth. In a curious twist, the Napoleon connection carried on through him. He happened to be stationed at Plymouth when HMS *Bellerophon* arrived with the fallen Emperor as its most celebrated passenger, and he found himself the conduit for conveying the Government's demands to him. History records he was not much impressed with his famous captive, whom he thought put on too many air and graces for a prisoner of war.

His wife, Jean, was an only child and an heiress to boot, so when she died in 1789, baby Margaret inherited the barony of Nairne. Unfortunately it was in attainder at the time because of her hedge-planting grandfather's support for the Jacobites.

Lady Bracknell famously remarked in *The Importance of Being Earnest* that to "lose one parent may be regarded as a misfortune; to lose both looks like carelessness". In 1823, Margaret was careless enough to lose her father as well as her mother and inherited his Meikleour estate, thereby becoming Baroness Keith. Finally, in 1837, on the death of her cousin, Margaret also became Lady Nairne. Titles seemed to drop into her lap as the gentle rain from heaven.

She was living in Paris in 1867 when she went to heaven, but before she did, she produced five daughters of whom Emily Jane, the one who employed David Bryce, was the first. In 1834, when she was only 15, Chopin, her tutor, dedicated his *Boléro* to her. (No greater love hath a tutor for his pupil than he compose a tune for her.)

When she grew up, Emily married Henry Petty-Fitz Maurice on 1st November 1843 at the British Embassy in Vienna. On his father's death in 1863, her husband became the 4th Marquess of Landsdowne and she, the Marchioness. On her mother's death in 1867, however, she was not able to succeed her as Baroness Keith as the title could only be passed down to male heirs. But in 1874, she was recognised by the House of Lords as the 8th Lady Nairne. She died at Meikleour House on 26th June in 1895, aged 76.

As I said above, it was she who commissioned the redesigning of Meikleour House and the Napoleonic connection continues in the drawing room, now part of the East Wing. It is named the "Empress'" bedroom after the Empress Eugenie (1826-1920), a frequent visitor. She was the wife of Napoleon III and the last Empress of France.

You can spend three nights in the East Wing, where you might be treated to a sight of the family heirloom: a lock of Napoleon's hair. There used to be a death mask too, but you are out of luck if such things are to your taste as it has been loaned to a museum.

If, on the other hand, catching your death by standing up to your nipples in cold water is more to your taste, then during your stay, you might like to try your luck in the River Ericht which is *hoaching* with the king of fish. It will only set you back £2,400 or so, although it does have five bedrooms and sleeps up to eleven people. You could ask the others to

Meikleour Village

chip in or hope at least, they would offer to make a contribution.

It's well worth, since you are so near, taking a slight detour along the Old Military Road, aka the present A984, to the pretty little village of Meikleour. There you will find the Meikleour Hotel built in 1820 as a staging post on the Inverness-Edinburgh route. Later it became a lodge for the shootin'-'n'-fishin' set. It's a more affordable option than the East Wing and also owned my Mr and Mrs Nairne, so if even if you are not a big spender, you can choose to spend a little time and money in the restaurant and bar – even if you don't stay the night.

Mercat Cross, Meikleour

In the centre of the village is the ring-fenced (by iron railings), Mercat Cross, where goods were bought and sold and farm workers were hired. The village was given burgh status in 1665, although it is thought the cross dates from 1698. The sands of time have certainly worn away the sandstone.

Across the road, standing in lonely isolation, and also fenced in as if it might abscond, is the Tron. The word comes from the Old French *tronel* or *troneau,* meaning a "balance" – the Weights and Measures Board of medieval times. A time, incidentally, before they were standardised and where they varied from village to village. The tron here takes the form of a standing stone with a hole in the middle like a prototype for a Henry Moore statue and in which the scales would have been balanced.

The Tron, Meikleour

It was also where thieves and miscreants were chained by the neck to an iron collar known as *jougs,* and where the whole village and visitors could come for a bit of a laugh as they pelted you with rotten eggs and vegetables like the coconut

Meikleour Arms

shy at a fairground today. Oh, the fun and the shame! A great deterrent, I would have thought, to stealing something... but what's a poor starving man to do to support his family in times of hardship and before the days of Universal Credit?

Just down the road a little bit, at the Meikleour Arms, a finger-post points the way to a mysterious feature concealed in the woods. It's called the "Cleaven Dyke", a grassy mound in a clearing. It's over a mile long, between 3 and 6 feet high and 30 feet wide. A couple of ditches run parallel on either side, about 20 feet wide wide and 4 feet deep. Obviously man-made and once erroneously thought to be a Roman *vallum*, or defensive wall, connected with the nearby Inchtutil Fort on the other side of the meandering Tay.

It's one thing to dig like an archaeologist to discover the past but it must have been another thing entirely to create the Cleaven Dyke. Imagine how many man-hours it must have taken to dig out those trenches, deeper and yet deeper, and building the mound up higher and yet higher. But the question is why? Why would anyone make all that back-breaking work for themselves on purpose? The present-day adage has it that "hard work never killed anyone", but I am not in the least convinced about that.

This monumental mound of earth is glorified by the name of a *cursus* and is very much overgrown with grass and bushes. What the builders actually called it (apart from whatever curses they used in those days), no-one knows, but one thing is for certain: whoever they were, they didn't speak Latin. Radiocarbon dating after an excavation in 1993 established that it was built before 3,600BC – but *why* they did so, even the experts can't enlighten us. Perhaps in the days before TV, it was merely a way of keeping the people occupied, such as Gulliver

Cleaven Dyke

found when he visited the Grand Academy of Lagado in Balnibardi where large numbers of people were engaged in such futile tasks as trying to extract sunbeams from cucumbers. The most likely explanation for the *cursus* however (and this is not the only instance of one in the UK), is that it was for some ceremonial purpose, now lost in the mists of time, but possibly to do with paying respect towards the ancestors.

There is another tumulus or Neolithic barrow near Inchtutil and another on the other side of the river, almost directly opposite. And if you look at an OS map you will find cairns, standing stones, hut circles and field systems scattered like a rash all over the landscape. It is a land that has been occupied since ancient times, so long ago that it makes the period of Roman occupation seem as if yesteryear. Perth Museum has a wide range of artefacts from both the Neolithic and Bronze ages – flint arrowheads, spearheads, knives and animal hide scrapers – whilst the Kelvingrove Museum in Glasgow has the jewel in the crown: a bronze axe and sword.

We take our leave of Meiklour on an unclassified road and come to Chapel of Lethendy. Nearby is the Tower of Lethendy (not to be confused with Lethendy House) which, like Topsy, has grown very much since the original tower house was built in 1570 by Sir David Herring or Heron. In addition to the eight-bedroomed house, the 39 acres of grounds include an 18-hole golf course, two tennis courts, two gate lodges, two cottages and a heated swimming pool.

At the time of writing, it is the subject of a High Court legal battle between the owner, a Russian oligarch, and the Kremlin to recover £570 million, the details of which I won't weary you with. The only reason I mention the mansion at all is because it contains a rather special Pictish stone from the 10th century. With a rounded top and tapering at the bottom (suitable for planting in the ground), it is nearly four feet tall, more than a foot wide, and about four inches thick.

It is rather damaged due to misuse over the centuries including serving as the lintel to the original staircase of the tower house. It has now been removed and put on display inside the house though there is little likelihood of you ever being able to clap eyes on it in the flesh, so to speak. The most in-

The path to the Cleaven Dyke

teresting face features an angel with outstretched wings hovering over a couple of clerics, beneath whom are a couple of musicians, one playing the harp and the other a triple pipe. There is a drum like a tom-tom between them and, at their feet, a small dog with a curly tail. Well, that's what the experts say it is, but the longer I look at it (online) the more I am convinced it is a pig.

Ardblair Stone Circle on the B947

There is another stone, built into the stairway of the tower and only partly visible, showing a figure dressed in late medieval clothing. Under the foot are the letters NBUL, part of the name "Turnbul". There was a Bishop of Glasgow from 1447-51 called William Turnbul, and it looks as if he could be the most likely suspect for being the person represented on the stone.

We continue our journey on the B947 towards Blairgowrie and in a short time come to the Ardblair stone circle, or rather drive through it. There are not many stone circles in the world you can say that about. It is alternatively known as the "Leys of Marlee", from the Gaelic *mor liae* meaning the "great stones". Rather neatly, there are three stones to the north and three to the south, ranging in height from four to six feet.

The road was built in 1858, following an ancient track over the moors, re-erecting two stones which had toppled over in the process. Unfortunately, in 1969 a lorry knocked one of them over, damaging it so severely it had to be pieced together with unsightly iron bars before being set up again in concrete. History repeated itself when another stone was hit by a lorry in 2008. I suppose they *are* rather close to the road, which is rather narrow at this point, and – to try and prevent a re-occurrence – reflective warning signs have been placed at either end of the circle to warn motorists of their presence.

Thus modern health and safety meets prehistory, but it seems to me it would have been a far, far better thing if the road builders had done a jink around them rather than driving a road straight through them.

Chapter Two

Blairgowrie and Rattray: Faith and Fruit

SO this is Blairgowrie and Rattray, where – like the movie directed by Robert Redford – a river runs through it. "It", not them, please note. The two towns became one by an Act of Parliament in 1928.

The river in question is the Ericht with Blairgowrie on the west side and the smaller Rattray on the east. The latter's name probably derives from the Gaelic *Raitear* or *Baile Raiteir*, meaning "fortress" or "village of the fort". The derivation of Blairgowrie is more straightforward. Translated from the Gaelic *Blàr Ghobharaidh,* it simply means the "Plain of Gowrie". Although smaller, Rattray claims to be the older, dating from the 12th century. In 1634, Charles I made George Drummond of Blair the baron of Blairgowrie and it became a burgh in 1809.

In between these times, of course, were the First and Second Jacobite Rebellions, extinguished finally – as all the world knows – at Culloden in April 1746, the last battle to be fought on British soil. Everyone also knows who emerged victorious. In the aftermath, a mighty fortress was built during 1748-57 near Ardersier, not so very far from the battle site. They called it "Fort George" and a mighty fortress it was; the latest thing in fort design, hunkering down behind massive ramparts and presenting nothing at all of a target for would-be attackers. With the benefit of hindsight, it paid much too much respect to defeated Charlie's bedraggled surviving supporters – they never ever tried to launch an attack.

After the '15, the Government recognised the importance of getting troops and supplies to trouble spots as quickly as possible. Roads were the answer, and General Wade was the man appointed to deliver them. Never since Roman times had they been so good in Scotland – though in the places where they have survived, you can see just what a bone-shaking journey it would have been, especially if you were in the back of a cart. Wade gets the credit for this

Blairgowrie

road network, but in actual fact he left Scotland in 1740 and it was his depute, Major Caulfeild [sic], who picked up the baton and ended up building many more miles of road than Wade ever did – but have you ever heard anyone talk about a "Caulfeild Road"?

He it was who was behind the road from Blairgowrie to Fort George via Braemar in the 1740s and, about the same time, extended it southwards to Coupar Angus, or at least improved the track that was there beforehand. Today we call that section the A923, while the major, northern part is now followed pretty much by the A93 and the A939. And that is our way, at least as far as Braemar. Thank you, Major Caulfeild.

It was also about this time that the towns were umbilically joined by a bridge, replacing the ferry that had run between Meikleour and Kinclaven since medieval times. Sadly, the bridge did not last. It was washed away in the 1840s, but quickly replaced with another. The present bridge has been widened to meet the requirements of today's traffic.

Beneath it flows the life-blood of the towns, the swift-flowing Ericht rushing to meet the Isla, which, in its turn, soon feeds the maw of the mighty Tay. The Ericht owes its existence to the melt waters of the Cairngorms and its pace made it ideal to power the new-fangled linen mills. By 1790, a hundred weavers were plying their trade in them.

Seventy years later there were no fewer than eleven mills along this stretch of water and the work force had expanded to 1,600. The countryside had become an industrial townscape. Eight mills turned flax into linen, while three produced jute. Then ten years later in 1870, a twelfth mill – the Keathbank jute mill – was added on the Rattray side. It boasted the largest water wheel in all of Scotland, and brought the number of people employed in the mills to almost 2,000. The population as a whole now numbered 4,000. Incredible to think that a century beforehand there had only been 400 souls!

The mills are gone now and today the area has become the centre of the soft fruit industry, especially raspberries and strawberries. (Other fruits are available.) You know you are getting near Blairgowrie when you see acres of polytunnels cladding the hillsides. From a distance they look like snow: well, it is the beginning of the Snow Roads, after all.

Unnatural they may be, but the tunnels extend the season from May until October. Nowadays the strawberries are grown on raised beds for which I know the backs of the pickers will be extremely grateful. When I was a boy, my father volunteered my services at our neighbour's market garden, and I know just how backbreaking bending so low for hours on end is. I did sustain myself with the odd juicy berry or two, I must admit.

At the same time my back was bearing the brunt of this unpaid employment in the north-east in the Fifties, here – in the heart of Scotland – pickers were being bussed in from Perth and Dundee, while at Essendy, near Lethendy, an encampment was set up for people from Glasgow who came to earn some pocket money during their summer holidays. It was called "Tin City" and was so extensive it had its own shops, even a chapel and post office.

The Wellmeadow and War Memorial, Blairgowrie

At its peak, a canning factory and a jam factory were built to process the fruit. They are gone now, like the railway which came in 1855 and which used to take the produce away, as well as the fruit pulp which would be turned into "jam tomorrow", as the White Queen in *Alice Through the Looking-Glass* might have put it.

At the present time, the bulk of the pickers come from Eastern Europe, and are accommodated in caravans on the particular farm where they are picking. Who will pick the fruit in the future remains to be seen.

Nowadays the town is geared towards the leisure industries, cashing in on the purses and wallets of those heading for the Glenshee Ski Centre. However, for those who prefer not to zip down a hillside at speeds of up to a hundred miles an hour but prefer instead to spoil a good walk by knocking the hell out of a little white ball, there are two 18-hole courses – and, if that were not quite enough already, there is a 9-hole course as well.

Not suffering from this addiction or affliction – call it what you will – we follow the riverside path upstream and come in a short time to Cargill's Leap. It is a very pretty walk, and worth going on for its own sake. The Rev. Donald Cargill, however, would not have had time to admire the scenery on one particular day during the Killing Time, far less "stop and stare" at the beauties of nature, as that Super-Tramp, W.H. Davies, urged us to do. Cargill was being hotly pursued by the dragoons for his adherence to the proscribed Presbyterianism.

There is a viewing platform from where, just downstream, you can see the spot where Cargill made his life-saving leap across the rocky gorge where the Ericht, brown-stained with peat, gushes through the narrow gap, swirling and eddying. Or did he? Far be it for me to spoil a good story, and in his lifetime he did have many close squeaks from capture up and down the land, but I have to point out it's not that narrow for a start – and, for another, I cannot find any historical record of the event. I leap to the conclusion therefore that this is more a case of a geographical feature in want of a name, similar to the "Soldier's Leap" at the River Garry at Killiekrankie where Donald MacBean made a death-defying leap in 1689 as he fled from the Jacobites after the Battle. And who more fitting than the local celebrity than he should lend his name to this gorge?

The Rev. Cargill was born in 1627 or 1628 at Nether Cloquhat on the Black Water near its confluence with the Ericht, and from the age of six or seven was brought up at Bonnington, just to the north of Rattray. Close enough for Rattray to claim him as its son.

If the story about Donald's leap to safety *is* true, it was only a stay of execution. His enemies finally caught up with him and hanged him high in Edinburgh on 27th July 1681. As he ascended the ladder to the scaffold, he turned to the crowd who had come to see such fun and addressed them thus: "The Lord knows I go on this ladder with less fear and perturbation of mind than ever I entered the pulpit to preach." Anyone who is unaccustomed to public speaking will know the feeling, but the truth is Donald was anything but unaccustomed to speaking to large crowds where they met in secret places to worship away from the prying eyes of the dragoons.

Cargill's Leap

If I can't take his farewell to the world entirely at face value, I can accept he truly believed he was just a short neck-stretch away from meeting his Maker in heaven. It must be a great thing to go to your death, and a nasty one at that, in the complete and utter faith that the best is yet to come. He was a man on the run with a price on his head, in constant fear of arrest. Yes, I can see how the grave must have seemed quite welcoming for it was a far, far better sleep he went to than he had known in a long time.

But to begin at the beginning, Donald's exciting life really kicked off in earnest on 29th May 1662. Two years earlier to the day, on his thirtieth birthday as it happens, Charles II returned from exile in Holland and entered London. A public holiday was declared and thanksgiving services were held throughout the length and breadth of the land. The event came to be known as "Oak Apple Day".

Two years later, it was clear to the Presbyterians, like Donald, that Charles II had no intention of carrying out the promise his father had made in the Solemn League and Covenant of 1643, which – amongst other pledges – was for "the extirpation of popery [and] prelacy". In actual fact, Charles was zealous in doing precisely the opposite.

And so it came to pass that on that day in May 1662, the bold Donald made a speech to his flock at the Barony Church in Glasgow. It was a speech that was to change his life and lead ultimately to his death. This is part of what he said:

> *We are not come here to keep this day upon the account for which others keep it. We thought once to have blessed the day wherein the king came home again, but now we think we shall have reason to curse it; and if any of you come here in order to the solemnising of this day, we desire you to remove.*

For these sentiments he was banished to "north of the Tay", where he joined the Covenanters and went on to draw large crowds when he preached at open-air meetings called "conventicles". He fought and was wounded at the Battle of Bothwell Bridge in June in 1679, but managed to escape. After he came back from exile in Holland, he wrote a document known as *The Queensferry Papers* in which he called for people to "overthrow the kingdom of darkness". He pulled off another narrow escape there on 3rd June 1680, but it was to be his last. In July of the following year he was captured at Covington near Biggar.

The rest you know.

Chapter Three

West of Blairgowrie:
A Fake, a Ghost and a Polymath

JUST to the west of the town, actually on its very fringe, is Newtown Castle, home of Sir William Macpherson (b. 1st April 1926) and, since 1969, 27th Chieftain of Clan Macpherson. A retired High Court Judge, he famously presided over the Stephen Lawrence trial and that of Robert Black, the serial child rapist and murderer. When he is at home and not wearing his blue *bunnet*, Sir William parks it on the head of a stuffed wildcat, *rampant*, which is very appropriate when you stop to think about it, as the clan crest features a wildcat, *sejant*, with the motto *Touch not the Cat bot a Glove*, where "bot" means "without".

The castle has been the family home of the Macphersons since 1787 when it was purchased by Alan Macpherson on the advice of James "Ossian" Macpherson (1738-96). The story behind the soubriquet is fascinating. When he was only 20, he had published *The Highlander*, an epic poem in six cantos. As later events turned out, he was honing his craft – greater things were to come.

In 1761 he began publishing *Fingal, an Ancient Epic Poem in Six Books, together with Several Other Poems composed by Ossian, the Son of Fingal, translated from the Gaelic Language*, and in 1765, a collected edition with the title *The Works of Ossian*. Fingal was an Irish mythological character aka *Fionn mac Cumhail* or Finn McCool; Ossian was a blind Scots bard who lived in the 3rd century. After the publication of his works, Macpherson became known as the *Homer of the North*. Thomas Jefferson called him the "greatest poet who ever lived", while Goethe compared him to Shakespeare. Great praise indeed but a greater achievement still, a more lasting legacy, is he inspired the Romantic Movement in poetry led by Wordsworth, Coleridge, and others.

The authenticity of the authorship was contested straight away by the historian Charles O'Connor, and later by Dr Johnson in his 1775 *A Journey to the Western Islands of Scotland* who alleged that Macpherson had fabricated his epic from fragments of Irish folk tales. The debate raged on well into the 19th century. Macpherson might have put the matter to bed for once and for all had he produced the originals but he never did, coming up with paper-thin excuses why he couldn't do so. He went to his grave never admitting that he was, in fact, "Ossian".

So why this modesty? Why this subterfuge? It may not explain everything, but the second Jacobite Rebellion had been put down only fifteen years previously and it in its aftermath came a whole raft of measures to snuff out Highland culture, such as the banning of the kilt and tartan. Was this a cunning plan by Macpherson to reintroduce Highland culture to the country at large by the back door, so to speak?

In any event, the extended poem certainly caught on – not just at home, but abroad, where, amazingly, it was translated into several languages including those of the more esoteric sort: Czech, Polish and Hungarian.

Macpherson died in 1796, just five months before Burns (a bad year for Scots poetry), and was buried in Westminster Abbey – not because of his literary achievements, but by his own wish, the Abbey being the local place of worship of one of his London residences. Ironically, his grave is not far away from his severest critic, Samuel Johnson – which just goes to show you that in death, like life, you don't always get everything you want.

One person who did not get what she wanted in life was Lady Jean Drummond of the castle who fell in love with the boy next door, one of the Blairs of Ardblair Castle, just one of the families with whom the Drummonds were feuding. It's an old, old story, most famously retold by Shakespeare in *Romeo and Juliet*, and like those star-crossed lovers, it did not end well. Heartbroken, the lady drowned herself in one of the nearby lochs. A Green Lady has been seen haunting the castle, a phenomenon so common amongst castles and stately homes up and down the land, it seems no self-respecting castle should be without one.

Another version, which does at least address the "green" in the ghost's name, is that she sought the help of a local "wise woman". She advised the lovelorn lady to cut grass from the churchyard, take a branch from the rowan tree that grew on the site of the gallows, bind them together and – at midnight – sit and wait for her suitor at the *Corbie Stane*, one of the many standing stones in the area.

She did as the old wife said and waited and waited. At long last she heard the sound of laughter, felt something tugging at her clothes and fell asleep – though if you ask me, I think it's more likely she fainted. When she awoke, gone was her gown of silk and satin, her shoon with silver buckles, and the pearls and jewels in her hair with which assets she had hoped to bedazzle him.

Instead, when she awoke at dawn, she found herself attired completely in green, the colour of the fairies.

Lord Ronald, the object of her desire, found her bewitching and, not long afterwards, they were married – her wedding dress being the aforesaid one of green. No sooner had they exchanged their vows when she became deathly pale and her hand felt deathly cold.

The outlook from Ardblair Castle

Uttering an unearthly scream, she fell to the ground, stone dead. They laid her out on what would have been the marriage-bed, and it is said that her gravestone turns around three times on Halloween. On that day she is also supposed to poke about the castle searching for Lord Ronald.

It is said to be connected by a secret tunnel to nearby (but not that near) Ardblair Castle, which is also a private residence. Both families were Jacobite sympathisers, so the story of the tunnel may well be true – a hiding place or an escape route from the Redcoats. If it *does* exist, no-one is telling, which is why it remains a secret. If only it had existed in Lady Jean's day and she had known about it, her story may have had a happier ending.

Ardblair began as a typical L-shaped tower with wings added in the 17th century, built upon where the walls of the courtyard or *barmkin* would have stood. Thus the courtyard shape is preserved, unusually for a Scottish castle, though the loch that once almost surrounded it (probably the reason why the original fort was built there as a natural defence) has nearly all been drained. Perhaps it's the very one where Lady Jean Drummond drowned herself in the alternative version of the story.

The tower itself was built on the site of a Norman fort, so it is said, by Alexander de Blair, a favourite of William the Lion, aka William I, aka William the Rough (reigned 1165-1214). It was pretty hard not to lose the head that bore the crown in those days. For trivia fans, he was the second-longest serving king of Scotland before the Union of 1707. (James VI would have been the longest, if the Union aforesaid had not intervened.)

Two centuries after Alexander, the lands of Ardblair were granted to Thomas Blair of Balthaycock, near Perth, in the reign of David II (1329-71). They were a bit of a murderous bunch back then, the Blairs. Patrick of that ilk was beheaded in 1554 for the murder of George Drummond of Ledcrieff and his son, William. Then, in 1562, the Blairs were asked to provide sureties or guarantees for the murder of Alexander Raa of Perth and "diverse other crimes".

In 1769, the 11th Laird of Ardblair died, leaving two daughters: Margaret and Christian. The latter married Laurence Oliphant, 8th Laird of Gask in 1759. Like his father before him, he was a fervent Jacobite, an aide-de-camp to Bonnie Prince Charlie no less, and who fought at the battles of Falkirk and Culloden before finally hanging up his musket in 1792. His daughter, Carolina (1766-1845), whom he named after his former boss, became Lady Nairne after she married her second cousin, Major William Murray Nairne, the 5th Lord Nairne in 1806.

She was a contemporary of Burns and became a famous lyricist in her own right. Amongst her compositions are as such standards as *Will Ye No' Come Back Again?* and *Charlie is my Darling*. She only began writing her lyrics nearly fifty years after Culloden, which tells you that they were a sentimental longing for what might have been.

The family are proud owners of the shoes Charlie wore when he escaped to Skye dressed up as Flora MacDonald's servant, Betty Burke. They also have his gloves, his spurs, his bonnet, his garter and not least, his crucifix, which I imagine he was particularly attached to.

Believe it or not, there was another lyricist in the family, namely Laurence's uncle, Thomas Oliphant (1799-1873), who was also a bit of a translator. Amongst his many credits are the English lyrics to *Men of Harlech, All Through the Night* and *The Ash Grove* from the traditional Welsh songs. Perhaps most famously (though I suspect not a lot of people know this), he wrote the words of that Christmas standard, *Deck the Hall(s) with Boughs of Holly*. And very appropriately too, since he was baptised on Christmas Day 1799 at Forgandenny, four miles south of Perth. It was in his stars that he should write the Christmas carol. He also wrote the chorale of the wedding of the future Edward VII and Queen Alexandra, music by Prince Albert. It was not the only royal event he marked with his words. In fact, he was popularly known as the "Poet of the Court".

Finally, Laurence Oliphant, his namesake's great-grandson (1829-1888), author, diplomat, traveller and Christian mystic – along with his father, Anthony – is credited with bringing tea to Ceylon after the coffee plantations were wiped out with "coffee rust". And where would tea-drinkers everywhere be today without them? Not least my grand-uncle, who was a tea-planter in Ceylon and who is buried in Colombo cemetery.

Further along the A923 from Ardblair, we pass Rae Loch, though it can't be seen from the road, followed shortly afterwards by the Loch of Drumellie or Marlee Loch, a wildlife reserve run by the Scottish Wildlife Trust. It has also been designated a Site of Special Scientific Interest (SSSI) and part of a Special Area of Conservation. Shortly after that, we come to the Loch of

Rae Loch

Clunie. In that loch there is an islet and on that islet there used to be an Iron Age crannog on which now stand the remains of a L-plan tower house built sometime between 1485 and 1514 by George Brown, the Bishop of Dunkeld, and which he primarily used as a hunting lodge.

Talking of which, the records show there was a castle on the western side of the loch utilised in 849AD by Kenneth MacAlpin (810-858AD), the first King of Scots (ruled from 843), for hunting in the nearby royal forest. A later record shows it was occupied by the English after the Battle of Dunbar in 1296 – not the same castle, naturally; probably a wooden motte-and-bailey affair and later replaced by one of more sturdy stone.

It too was abandoned for a more secure location on the island in the late 15th century, but whose blocks and stones provided a very handy quarry for Bishop Brown's castle. In 1507, a chapel, St Catherine's, was built next to the tower. The interior was remodelled during the 18th century and a new kitchen range was built over the site of the chapel. The end came in the 20th century when it was gutted by fire and never rebuilt.

In 1560, a seismological event took place that would have shaken Bishop Brown to the core, and did shake the Catholic church to its foundations – the Reformation. Gone were the bishops, and the abbey lands passed into secular control. However, the wily last Bishop of Dunkeld, Robert Crichton – seeing the way the wind was blowing, and before his death in 1585 – granted the castle to his kinsman and namesake, Robert Crichton, Lord Advocate of Scotland. He married Elizabeth Stewart who, in the same year as the Reformation, bore him a son named James and from whom he could claim royal descent.

He grew up to be a bit of a polymath – languages, the arts and here's the thing, in the sciences too. He was fluent in no fewer than twelve languages from Arabic to the obscure Syriac, along with Hebrew and

Loch of Drumellie

Latin. After a career as a soldier in the French army, he finally ended up in the service of the Duke of Mantua. He was not to know it, but it was a fatal career move. The Duke's son, Vincenzo Gonzaga, was extremely jealous of him, partly because his father admired Crichton so much, and not least because his mistress dumped him for Crichton.

As he left her dwelling one night, Crichton was attacked by three masked men. He was an expert fencer, as well as horseman, singer, musician, debater and orator. (Was there nothing the man could not excel at?) Three against one. No problem for Crichton. He defeated them and the ringleader was unmasked as none other than Vincenzo. It was more than his life was worth to run his employer's son through with his sword, so what was he to do? Brainbox he may have been, but Crichton underestimated the depth of Vincenzo's jealousy and hatred. He dropped to one knee and presented the hilt of his sword to him, whereupon Vincenzo drove the blade straight through Crichton's heart. Hell hath no fury like a defeated rival in love.

That said, the account of his death, like Mark Twain's, might be greatly exaggerated – as well as many of the details of his life. That eccentric and fellow polymath, Sir Thomas Urquhart (1611-60), published an account of his life in 1652 called *The Jewel*. If there is one thing that can be said about his prose style, it is that he was much addicted to hyperbole, so the reader would be well advised to take the details of Crichton's life and death with a good dose of salt.

Nevertheless, it *is* true he was a man of distinction, and his reputation lives on in *Crichton* by the historical novelist, Harrison Ainsworth (1837), in Thackeray's *Vanity Fair* (1847), in Dickens's *The Haunted House* collection of short stories (1859), in Trollope's *The Prime Minister* (1876)... but most famously, of course, by J.M. Barrie who used the soubriquet in his satirical comedy *The Admirable Crichton* (1902).

That's an admirable legacy.

Chapter Four

Alyth: The Arches, the Instrument Maker and the Drunks' Cart

THE Snow Roads, in my book, is a means to an end, not the be-all and end-all. It's a road, not a railroad that you must follow where the tracks take you, and having come all this way from our home in central Scotland, I'm not going to pass up the opportunity to do a little off-piste sight-seeing should the opportunity present itself. And it does, which is why we are heading east on A926 from Rattray instead of heading for the hills on the A93.

In a very short time we arrive in the charming little village of Alyth, from the Gaelic *Àilt* or *Allaid* meaning a "rock". To the northeast of the town, on top of Barry Hill (short for Barrow), there are the collapsed ramparts of a Pictish fort, where – according to legend – King Mordred kept Queen Guinevere prisoner. We will come back to her and her story in a little later when we go to Meigle. In the meantime, myth though that may be, it is a fact that there was a church in Alyth from the 6th century dedicated to St Molaug of Lismore, the patron saint of Argyll.

He is a new saint on me, but there are more saints in the Catholic hagiography than you can shake a crozier at. He was born in what is now Northern Ireland sometime before 520 and died in 592, thus making him not only very long-lived for those times, but a contemporary of arguably the most famous saint in Scottish history, St Columba. (Is he happy in heaven, hiding his halo under a bushel,

Alyth

content with his relative anonymity, or is he secretly jealous of his contemporary's super-saint stardom, even although he knows envy is number six in the list of deadly sins?)

Another church was built on the site in the 12th century and Robert the Bruce is said to have popped in for a bit of a pray in 1326 when he was hunting deer in the local forests. And well he needed to get on his bended knees, for – as everyone knows – he had committed murder, a terrible sin to be sure, but his was doubly so since he had committed the dreadful deed in a church resulting in him being excommunicated. It doesn't get much worse than that for a medieval criminal, or even a good person in medieval times. I can well believe he took every opportunity to pray for his immortal soul and maybe it worked – who knows? – for two years later, Pope John XXII rescinded his excommunication. When Bruce heard the news it was probably the best night's sleep he had had in a long time. As everyone knows, hell's fires are as hot as a crematorium oven, the difference being they are never quenched.

The Arches, Alyth

In the cemetery which the locals call "The Arches", three mighty Romanesque red sandstone arcs are propped up in their old age by two mighty iron girders. The arches date from 1500 and once formed the northern side of the aisle that ran down the nave of the medieval church. Nothing remains of the matching south side. The gates of the cemetery are padlocked but you can see, through the bars, at the eastern end of the arches and in the oldest and surviving part of the church, two aumbries (cupboards in which the sacramental vessels were kept): one square and, next to it, another with a pointed arch. According to the noticeboard, there is a third aumbry, and while things do tend to come in threes, I can no sign of it from where I'm standing.

The cemetery is the resting place of several local worthies, notably James Sandy Jr. who used to live in what is now the Alyth Arms, formerly called the Commercial Inn and built by his father, a master mason, around 1722.

His life was dogged by bad luck. When he was twelve, he fell on ice and damaged one leg so badly he was unable to walk on it again. Then, so the story goes, when he was sixteen, the Alyth Burn burst its banks and flooded the Inn. As his mother was trying to drag him to safety upstairs, she lost her grasp and his other leg was broken so badly he was crippled in that leg too, poor chap. His

The Alyth Arms

legs may have been functionless but he was very good with his hands – a talented craftsman, in fact.

A special couch was constructed with raised sides to hold his tools which included lathes, vices and a circular saw. From here he held court and made a wide range of objects such as artificial limbs and false teeth; optical instruments; farm implements; spinning wheels; and clocks and musical instruments including a set of bagpipes. But what he is remembered for best of all is the invention of a snuffbox with a hidden hinge which not only kept out the grains of snuff but made it airtight. I believe such a thing was vitally important. A board attached to the first floor of the "Arms" proclaims the young James's achievements.

Aged fifty-three, he decided to get married. Silly Sandy. I do not know if his new wife wore him out or not but, at any rate, he died only nineteen days later, on 3rd April 1819. That lesser-known poet, but commonly-named man, John Smith, penned some lines to Sandy's memory which includes these lines:

> *Dirks an' sowards, bows an' arrows*
> *Magic mirrors, wheels for barrows*
> *Traps an' cages, singin' sparrows*
> *Scapes for bees.*
> *Model cairts, an' pleughs an' harrows*
> *He made wi' ease.*

His achievements were many and remarkable, but what tickles me most is that as on his couch he lay making all these objects, he multi-tasked by hatching songbirds' eggs with the heat of his body and then kept them as pets.

Another person of note who is sleeping the Big Sleep in the cemetery is Sir George Ramsay, 6th Baronet of Bamff. He is worthy of mention because he was one of the last people in Scotland to be killed in a duel with a certain Captain Macrae at Musselburgh on 16th April 1790. A dubious honour to be sure, but everyone has to die of something and you may as well die of something for which you'll be remembered – except I never had heard of him until now, and so too have you now. You did not die in vain, Sir George!

There is a funerary monument to him in the new church which was completed in 1839 and designed by Thomas Hamilton of Edinburgh, he who designed the Burns Monument in Edinburgh, the Martys' Monument on Calton Hill and many, many more. Its spire towers above the church like a finger pointing towards the place to which many aspire when they are no more.

Inside there are two interesting features of note. Firstly, in the porch, a Pictish carved stone from the late 7th century or early 8th greets you. One side has a decorated cross whose swirling loops are thought to represent life everlasting (where do the loops begin and end?). It has a shaft or handle at the bottom, indicating that it was intended to be carried about at the head of a procession.

The other side – the back-side, if you pardon the expression – bears the mysterious double disc and Z-rod so typical of Pictish symbolism, and therefore shows the fusion between paganism and Christianity. It was discovered in 1887 when work was going on in the church lands, or glebe.

It's not the only Pictish stone that Alyth can boast. Another stands in a field on Bruceton Farm slightly to the east of the town. What's special about it is that it has not moved from the spot where it was erected all those centuries ago. Those who know about such things think it is probably a grave marker. So, should you pay a visit, please tread softly so as not to disturb his dreams. He must have been a man of some importance in his day for them to have gone to such an enormous effort to lug that massive stone to the top of the hill, and no small matter either to raise it to the vertical. Rest in peace whoever you are – but beware, archaeologists are not just roaming the earth: they are digging it up.

They did exactly that at nearby Shanzie Farm after the cruel coulter passed through a C-shaped late Iron Age cell or souterrain, damaging it in the process. It did, however, provide the archaeologists with an opportunity to get to work with their spades and trowels. The structure was crescent-shaped, 115 feet long, and it contained a single chamber 50 feet long. At the best-preserved part, where the walls were three or four courses high, the archaeologists noted they were starting to corbel inwards, indicating that the roof was capped with stone rather than timber. It

Alyth Church

Alyth Old Bridge

is thought they were used for storage or as a hiding place from attackers, not a place to bury the dead.

I don't know how they know, but the archaeologists tell us it had been broken into twice – once during the medieval period and again during Victorian times. The looters didn't take everything, however. They left behind some pottery, both prehistoric and Roman, a quern stone fragment, an amber ring, two copper alloy rings, a brooch and a pair of tweezers.

Back in the present, if it is true to say that a river runs through Blairgowrie, then it is equally true to say that a burn runs through Alyth on its way to meet the River Isla. In fact, that is what gives it its charm; more particularly, the packhorse bridge that crosses it. It is thought to have been built between 1480 and 1514 so when you walk across it, you are stepping back in history, treading in the footsteps of millions of others who have used the very same bridge for five centuries. In 1488, James III raised Alyth to the status of a Burgh of Barony, thus giving it the right to hold fairs and markets. The bridge was heightened and parapets added in the 19th century. (Note the wedge-shaped piers to deflect the flow of the water and break up ice.)

Alyth may be smaller than Blairgowrie now but back then it was by far the bigger settlement. By the middle of the 18th century, it was holding as many as nine fair days a year, or at least it did so on one notable occasion. Dismiss dodgems and merry-go-rounds from your mind, gentle reader. This was all about horse-trading in both the literal and metaphorical sense – selling whatever you had to sell – such as yourself, as a farmhand. Think of Thomas Hardy and the opening to *The Mayor of Casterbridge*, though to the best of my knowledge in Alyth, no wives were sold to the highest bidder.

If you would like to try

The Losset Inn, Alyth

and imagine the village as it was those times, then you need look no further than the Losset Inn, an old drovers' inn built in 1760. It stands at the bottom of Toutie Street, so named because the herdsman would toot on his way to and from pasture, like that enthusiastic pioneering motorist Mr Toad in *Wind in the Willows* – not to warn people to run for their lives, but to let the owners know to bring out their cow or come and collect it. I would have thought that the lowing they made would have been enough to have awakened not just babies but every person on the street and there was thus no need to toot.

Ancient deeds show that the occupants of more than 200 properties were allowed the right to graze their cow on Alyth Hill to the north and Market Muir to the south. But just where did the villagers keep their milk cow, or cows? That's what I'd like to know! And there's more. Most of them kept half-a-dozen sheep as well. Self-sufficiency was the order of the day.

Times change and so, of course, so did Alyth. Looking at this idyllic little place now, it is hard to imagine it was once home to two linen mills. Small beer to Blairgowrie, as you know, and its little burn was no match for the more forceful Ericht rushing madly to its rendezvous with the Tay. The railway came in 1861, aiding and abetting the textile industry, so that by 1870 there were 350 people earning their living in the mills. A carpet factory used to trade as late as the 1990s, but that too has gone and been replaced by a company restoring vintage cars. *And so it goes*, as Kurt Vonnegut said (several times) in *Slaughterhouse-Five*. I think there is a certain neatness in the notion of the past being replaced by the more recent past for the foreseeable future.

Alyth Museum

If you want to learn more about Alyth, then the small (but perfectly formed) museum will tell you about its industrial and agricultural past, with pictures. Everyone has heard of the Glasgow Boys and perhaps some have heard of the Glasgow Girls, but hands up – who has heard of the Blairgowrie Boys? To be honest I hadn't either, and it was only thanks to the Alyth museum that I have now and whose top floor is dedicated to an exhibition of their works.

They centre around the self-taught William Geddes (1840-84) and his son, Ewan (1866-1936). William was mainly a painter of fish (well it takes all kinds), while Ewan was a water colourist who painted the Perthshire landscape in all its infinite variety. There was also another son, Robert Smith Geddes (aka Bob, 1883-1951), who dabbled a bit and trained at Edinburgh School of Art, but gave it up and emigrated to Canada. Ewan regarded him as being more talented than he. If so, it's a pity he didn't stick at it. But then artists, in the broadest sense of the word, tend to be a bit temperamental.

Also on the top floor is an interesting cart. It's like an elongated narrow wheelbarrow, just big enough to carry a body, and you might be forgiven for thinking it was some sort of open bier. The truth is a bit more interesting, though if you did think "bier" you weren't so far out – it was used to carry those who had imbibed too liberally of alcoholic refreshment back home to their ever-loving wives. It even has a wooden headrest, though – that said – it wouldn't have been the last word in comfort. You would have to have been dead drunk to have submitted yourself to that sort of bone-shaking journey home over the cobbles, but it was probably nothing to the tongue-lashing they got when they were delivered back home.

They don't provide that sort of service any more, but in other respects some things never change.

Chapter Five

Meigle and Coupar Angus: Stories in Stones

AND so it is time to take our leave of Alyth, which we do on the B952. At the roundabout shortly afterwards, it morphs into the B954 and takes us to Meigle. But we're not stopping there just yet. Instead we take a minor road towards the village of Ardler, but before which we come to Belmont Castle, not to be confused with the residence of the *lady richly left*, as Shakespeare fans will automatically think of when they hear the name.

It is a mansion all right, but doesn't look in the least Italian. And why should it, being in the depths of the Perthshire countryside?

It started off as a three-storey tower house, complete with shot holes, called Kirkhill of Meigle. It was owned by the Bishops of Dunkeld who lived like lords of the manor high above the hoi polloi in their 16th century skyscraper. Then came along came a man called Martin Luther and, in the fullness of time, the tower house and the lands were sold off. Eventually, in the mid 18th century, they came into the hands of James Stuart-Mackenzie who built the castle which incorporated the old tower.

It was remodelled in the late 19th century and was once the home of Sir Henry Campbell-Bannerman, Prime Minister of these Isles from December 1905 until his death of heart failure aged 72 at 10 Downing Street on 22nd April 1908. He has the distinction of being the first person to officially bear the

Belmont Castle

title of "Prime Minister" and, less enviably, the only PM to have died at the official residence. He is buried in the cemetery at Meigle where there is a plaque to his memory on the exterior north-east wall of the church.

Once upon a time you could have lived in Belmont too, just as long as you satisfied the age test. It's too late now. Until 2013, it served as an old folks' home run by the Church of Scotland. Today it has a forlorn sort of air, which – to my mind – has shades of the prison house about it with its tall chimneys, turrets, row upon row of severe unseeing windows, cold grey stone (host to a prolific growth of lichen), but most of all to the entrance door which looks much more like the gateway to one of the places where guests are detained at Her Majesty's pleasure, and very far removed from what the entrance to a stately home should look like.

We drive back to the road, and soon we come to the lodge where there are acres of space to park. From there, rising tall above a stone wall, we can see what we have come out of our way to see – but how we are going to get to it? The only way seems to lies ahead down a phalanx of rhododendrons.

Before too long a gap appears and, threading our way through the bushes, we emerge into a green sward at the end of which is the impressive monolith known as the "Macbeth Stone". That indefatigable early travel writer, naturalist and antiquarian, Thomas Pennant (1726-1798), came here in 1776 and wrote that it was a monument to "brave young Seward, who fell, slain on the spot by MacBeth [sic]". He went on to say it is 12 feet high, just over 18 feet in girth at its thickest part, 32 inches of it are below ground and it weighs 20 tons. Legend has it that a stone coffin was found buried at its base, but no sign of it has been seen since it was supposedly exposed.

The Macbeth Stone

What Pennant does not mention, but which Sir James Simpson does a century later, is the presence of cup-marks on both sides. Eight years later, in 1884, Thomas Wise not only described them, but drew them as well. In his *History of Paganism* he tells us (erroneously) that the stone stands on the spot where Macbeth was slain. The cup-marks, of different sizes and grouped randomly, run round the boulder about three feet above the ground. Since it faces south-east, he concludes it was used for some sacred purpose.

Most of the cup-marks are quite hard to make out now, being very much covered with lichen. We are told there is possibly one on the north face, two on the south and twenty-four on the western side, but the majority are on the east which has forty, most of them clustered about the middle. That side is smooth and flat, giving the stone – as whole – a wedge-like appearance.

Also pretty hard to make out is a face-like feature at the top, though once you have seen it, it is hard to dismiss it again. With huge cavities like empty eye sockets, it seems to stare inscrutably into the distance like one of those statues on Easter Island. Was that why this particular stone was chosen by the people who erected it? Perhaps they thought it had magical powers and was the focus for some sort of ritual connected with ancestor worship.

Whatever the truth of that may be, according to local folklore, it was a meeting place for witches. Well, where else would they meet given the pivotal part they played in the Scottish play? Perthshire is *Macbeth* country after all: *high Dunsinane hill*, Birnam Wood and Glamis are only a short broomstick ride away and you will not have forgotten that at the start of the play, before he disposed of King Duncan, Macbeth was Thane of Glamis.

Unfortunately the monolith has been the target of vandals. The name SCOTT has clearly been carved out at some point in the past by someone with some skill with the chisel – not your typical sort of graffiti. Beneath that another name has been executed in much cruder lettering, which is difficult to make out and which I won't repeat here so as not to glorify the vandal. It's crude and it's rude to deface an ancient stone like this. Some people just have no respect.

On Forfar Road in rose-red Meigle (the colour of the local sandstone), there stands an ordinary-looking house but which bizarrely bears three sets of coats of arms, the likes of which you would expect to see on a stately home or a castle. What are they doing there? I am indebted to Canmore, the archaeological branch of Historic Environment Scotland (HES), for shedding some light on the mystery.

The Coats of Arms House, Meigle

On the gable end, the letters EB and WF are intertwined,

Coat of Arms: Detail

surrounded by the words YIS.HOVS.IS.BVLDS then after a space it resumes with EL-ESOBETH.BETOVN and at the bottom, the initials L.FVLLER-TOVN. Elizabeth was most likely the daughter of Robert Bethune of Balfour who married David Lindsay in 1609 and died in 1666.

To the right of the front door is the coat of arms of the Balfour and Beaton families whilst on the left is that belonging to the Fullerton family. It bears the initials WF, probably William Fullerton who married, circa 1648, Margaret, eldest daughter of Elizabeth and David aforesaid. I find the coat of arms rather amusing. In the top left and lower right quarters are three birds, painted red – or are they rabbits? It reminds me of the 1892 drawing in a German magazine which humorously posed the question "Which animals look most like each other?" Seen one way, the drawing looks like a rabbit, but look at it another way and what you see is a duck. It was used by Wittgenstein in his *Philosophical Investigations* to demonstrate two different ways of seeing: seeing *that* and seeing *as*.

What *I* am now beginning to see, in the comprehending sense of the word, is how these carved and painted stones came to adorn this house. Fullarton Castle was built at the end of the 15th century and in the time-honoured fashion, stones from it were used to build a farmhouse and steading in the mid-19th century, and it is from the latter that the stones somehow found their way into the fabric of the present house.

Turning to the House of God, the present church in Meigle was built in 1870, replacing an earlier building which burned down in 1793. But long before that, legend has it there was a church here built by monks from Iona in the early 600s. No trace of that remains (if it ever did exist), nor are there any remains of the medieval church which was built about 1400. One thing is certain, however: Christianity here has a long pedigree.

And now the time has come to tell the story of Guinevere which I promised you in the last chapter. In the cemetery there is a grassy hump known as "Vanora's Mound" which, as a little plaque points out, is said to be the grave of Guinevere who, you may remember, was allegedly kept captive by the Pictish King Mordred in his fortress on Barry Hill near Alyth. In an attempt to cover up her identity, she changed her name to Vanora.

As for Mordred, his parentage and story is complicated. Some sources say he was King Arthur's son, some say he was his nephew, while still others say he was the product of an incestuous liaison between Arthur and his half-sister, Morgause, Queen of Orkney. Whatever the case may be, he is credited with betraying Arthur (who was on his way to Rome preparatory to going on a crusade) – not just by making love to the Queen, who may also have been his mother (which adds extra spice to the tale), but by revealing Guinevere's affair with Lancelot, he managed to spark off the war whereby he hoped to depose Arthur and seize the crown. In the end, some say Arthur killed Mordred, some say it was the other way about, while a third version has it that they managed to kill each other. Take your pick.

But I get ahead of myself. When Vanora, or Guinevere, was released, far from being overjoyed to see her again, Arthur accused her of infidelity and sentenced her to death. But no ordinary death. She was put in a pit and pulled apart by starving dogs, the Pictish punishment for an adulterous woman. What the dogs didn't eat is under the mound.

Another version of the tale is that Guinevere was a willing captive of Mordred and it was the local people who put her to death, morally outraged by her scandalous behaviour. Not only that: as they cast her bits into her grave, they heaped curses upon her. I suppose you could say they didn't like her very much. To this day it is said that if a virgin walks over the mound she will be sterile. A load of nonsense, of course, but who – if she would like to be a mother – is brave enough to put it to the test?

Far be it from me to spoil a good story, but this horrendous death is most likely based upon a misreading of one of the carvings on an eight-foot high Pictish cross which rejoices under the name of "Meigle 2" and which shows on the reverse side, a figure surrounded by four animals which have a mean and hungry look, as if they mean to rip the figure to shreds. What it actually represents is Daniel in the lions' den, though to be fair, it does look as if he is wearing a dress. There is one snag with this story however, which as anyone who remembers their Sunday school stories can tell you, is that Daniel was not torn to shreds by the lions, but saved by divine intervention. That said, what the image on the stone may show is the moment before the miracle and I bet the lions were pretty pissed off with missing their meal as you can see their tongues are actually already licking him in anticipation of a tasty treat.

This stone, and others, can be seen in the Sculptured Stone Museum which is located in the old school behind the church. Now in the care of Historic Environment Scotland, it houses a collection of 26 Pictish stones, mostly coming from the cemetery. They are remarkably well preserved, and the standard of carving is exceptionally high. A group once stood on Verona's mound but that is not necessarily where they (or the others) were originally placed. Some fragments were found in the walls of the church, shamelessly broken to suit requirements. At least, in their bits and pieces, they survived. When the church caught fire in 1869, others were lost in the conflagration.

The stones span two centuries from the late 8th century to some youngsters from the late 10th. As well as cross-slabs, there are recumbent gravestones and one example of a hogsback gravestone (so called because it resembles a pig's back) which shows a Viking influence with its shingled "roof" and serpent on top. That's very interesting, but to me more interesting still are the mysterious symbols: mirrors and combs, double discs, Z-rods and V-rods. Then there is a whole menagerie of animals – lions, bears, bulls, horses, hunting hounds, dogs, snakes, serpents, seahorses that dance, a salmon, a griffin, an otter and even a camel. There are also mythical and fantastic beasts – the so-called "swimming elephant" or "Pictish Beast" and the deadly man-eating manticore with its lion's body, human face and scorpion's tail.

Meigle Sculptured Stone Museum

The Daniel Stone at Meigle Sculptured Stone Museum

What does it all mean? The Picts left no words of explanation behind them and, I have to say, I rather like that. You know the feeling you get after a conjuror's trick is revealed and you feel so stupid to have been taken in like that. You would prefer not to know. Similarly, I suspect if we knew for certain what the Pictish symbols and mythological creatures meant, we might feel a little bit disappointed.

The Picts also left another mystery behind them – where did they go? Where are they now? As it happens, we *do* know the answer to that one, just as you may remember from your schooldays that the name "Picts" was not a name they called themselves but was bestowed upon them by the Roman invaders on account of they way they painted their bodies to make themselves look fiercer in battle. I can see their point – I often feel intimated by the multi-coloured tattoos I happen to see in the streets and in the supermarket.

So, where *did* they go? The short answer is that many of their warrior chiefs were wiped out by the Vikings and they formed a coalition with the Scots of Dál Riata against the common enemy. Eventually, they were absorbed by the Scots under their king, Kenneth MacAlpin, and along with him were converted to Christianity – hence the crosses and biblical scenes. The Picts may be gone, but they will never be forgotten as long as their stones remain.

And if you still haven't had your fill of Pictish stones, then four miles away to the east, on the road to Forfar, you can see the finely-carved Eassie Stone which is dated to the late 7th century and which stands in a corner of the ruined church. It is protected from the elements by a shelter which was erected in 1987.

It is nearly 7 feet tall and just over 3 feet wide. It was found in the nearby burn by the Reverend Cordiner about 1786 and placed in the church yard around 1842. Probably it was chucked in the burn (if that's the *mot juste* for something as heavy as this) just after the Reformation, when the depiction of religious images was regarded as idolatrous. On the cross side there is an angel and a figure facing it, with below them another person, a stag, an animal with its tail between its legs and a hunting hound. On the back, which has suffered quite a bit of weathering, there are the usual symbols, as well as a tree in a pot with three cloaked men making towards it, a man with a rod on his shoulder standing with his back to it, a horseshoe shape beneath it, and three cattle. What does it all mean? Well, it has been suggested that it might represent *Genesis 18* where three men or angels met Abraham at an oak tree. One scholar thinks that what appears to be growing on the tree are actually human heads. I think he may have a point. On the other hand they could be apples. Nobody really knows.

The A94 takes us to Coupar Angus, so named to distinguish it from Cupar in Fife. It became a burgh in 1607, which gave it the right to hold fairs and markets. A stream runs through it too, and it once formed the boundary between Angus and Perthshire. The town really should be called "Coupar Perthshire", as the boundary has now moved three miles further east. It has absolutely nothing at all to do with a shift of the tectonic plates but has everything to do with upheavals in local government. Good idea to keep the name the same, though. The more geographically accurate name doesn't come quite so trippingly off the tongue.

In 1164, Malcolm IV (reigned 1153-65), founded a Cistercian monastery here which was manned by monks from Melrose. Malcolm was only twelve when he came to the throne and only twenty-four when he died in his bed, probably of cancer. He was a weak king, both physically as well as a ruler, forced to kowtow to the much mightier Henry II of England. As a consequence, he was rather unkindly given the soubriquet of *Malcolm the Maiden* – which, sadly for Malcolm, does slip rather easily off the lips. That's what alliteration does for you.

As for the monastery, which was blessed with the name of the "Abbey of the Blessed Virgin Mary of Coupar", it was an early victim of the Reformation, being destroyed by a mob in 1559. It limped on in its damaged state until the death of the last monk in 1606 when the abbey lands were granted to James Elphinstone, Lord Coupar. Only part of a gatehouse now remains, heavily propped up by timbers and fenced off for safety reasons. The rest of the stones enjoyed a second life as building material for the growing town.

The most obvious reuse can be seen in the new church nearby which was built in the 1800s and which houses some of the monastery's carved stones and tombs, and the six-storey Tolbooth down the street a little way. It was built as a meeting place for the burghers in 1762 and paid for by public subscription. A plaque above a tiny window (which bizarrely has two iron bars in the form of a cross in front of it) attests to this fact and also tells us that it was a "Prison of Court of Regality" – that is to say an area of jurisdiction set up by the king and presided over by a lord of regality who had the same amount of power as a sheriff on both civil and criminal matters. These courts were abolished in 1746 in the aftermath of the Jacobite rebellion, as it was thought it gave the clan chief too much power over his tenants.

But back to the monastery. A ley tunnel is said to run from it to a souterrain at Pictur, two-and-a-half miles away. These tunnels are common in folklore, a matter of myth as often as not, and are said to link important buildings such as castles, stately homes and monasteries. (You will recall we have already come

Ruins of Coupar Angus Abbey

across such an example supposedly linking the castles of Ardblair and Newtown.)

I have been aware of secret passages and escape routes from castles since my Enid Blyton days, as have countless others, but as far as *this* tunnel is concerned, it is no mere fiction but a fact – though whether it extends as far as Pictur is another matter. In the 19th century, two women happened to find the entrance and went in. Only one returned. The other was never seen again. Then in 1982, a workman rediscovered the entrance and ventured inside. He only managed to get so far before he came across the collapsed roof of the tunnel. It looked as if he had also stumbled across the solution to the mystery of the missing woman.

Near Pictur, up on a ridge of the Sidlaw Hills, five hundred feet above sea level and overlooking the Strathmore Valley, stands the Keillor Symbol Stone. Over six feet in height and nearly three feet wide, it is a bit of a landmark and due to its exposed position, has been pretty much at the mercy of the weather, not to mention being a host for rampant lichen. It is carved on one side only and features a double disc and Z-rod in the middle, a mirror and possibly a comb below, while on the top is a carving of an animal, probably a wolf. The base was excavated in 1856, uncovering cist graves and a rickle of bones.

In the 19th century, Coupar Angus earned its living by spinning jute, linen, flax and hemp. The railway came in 1837 and bore the products away to market. In 1855, a branch to Blairgowrie connected Coupar Angus to the wider world – to Perth, Forfar and Aberdeen. It was all over by 1965 however, and the tracks were taken up in 1982. There was no going back.

The Tolbooth, Coupar Angus

But before *we* go back to Blairgowrie and back on the Snow Roads, it's interesting to note that Coupar Angus has produced one person of notoriety. Born in 1804, William Nairne Clark emigrated to Western Australia in 1830 on the good ship *Eliza* – a convict ship – as a passenger. On the morning of 6th June 1832, at Freemantle, he fought the first recorded duel in Australia, fatally wounding his opponent, George French Johnson. He was arrested, charged with manslaughter and acquitted. A lawyer to trade, he founded the *Swan River Guardian* in 1836. He died in Hobart, Tasmania, in 1854.

You could say he led an adventurous life after he left the sheltered confines of Coupar Angus. Is it better to stay safe and sound at home or risk a little excitement by venturing abroad? I am with Mr Clark. You can't say you have really lived at all until a little adventure, or misadventure, falls into your life.

Chapter Six

Blairgowrie to Finegand: A Tale of a Cockerell

WE'RE leaving Blairgowrie and Rattray now and heading for the hills on the A93. We are doing it the easy way by car, but those who are fond of a long walk can take the Cateran trail which is 64 miles long. The official start and finish is at Blairgowrie, but – since it is circular – you can join it anywhere. It is named after the Caterans, Central Scotland's equivalent of the Border Reivers who went about stealing cattle in the Highlands from the Middle Ages to the 17th century.

The trail follows the old drove roads across farmland and moors and through forests, taking in places like Bridge of Cally, Spittal of Glenshee, Alyth and Bamff – which is not to be confused with your narrator's place of birth, Banff, and which sounds exactly the same. It is said to be an easy five-day walk, but for the less energetic, or with less time to spare, there is a short-cut across country between Kirkmichael and Cray.

Six miles from Blairgowrie on the A93 is Bridge of Cally. The bridge aforesaid crosses the River Ardle just prior to it joining the Black Water, just before they both flow into the Ericht. Doing things in threes seems to be what Bridge of Cally does. Apart from the three rivers, it's at the head of three glens: Glenshee, Strathardle and Glenericht. It has a hotel, a post office, a village hall and not much more. The church at Netherton, a little to the north, closed in 2010, and the one-teacher school at Strone of Cally did likewise in 2011. However, on the posi-

The Bridge of Cally Hotel

tive side, there is a large holiday park – the village's *raison d'etre*, a sort of base camp for the skiing slopes of Glen Shee.

We unexpectedly find ourselves passing the entrance to it, as to our dismay, just after crossing the bridge, we see that the A93, the road to the Snow Roads is closed, not due to snow, but because of road works. In actual fact, it turned out to be a stroke of luck, for not only is the diversion on the A924 up Strathardle very scenic, but we otherwise would have missed the utterly charming humpbacked bridge on the B950 at Kirkmichael. It was a short detour and well worth taking it just to see the bridge.

Shortly after crossing it, we rejoin the A93 and head north up Glen Shee, from the Gaelic *Gleann Sith* meaning the "glen of the fairies". A glance at the OS map shows the landscape on both sides of the road, but especially to the east, heavily dotted with hut circles and field systems. What this represents is a great leap forward in the history of mankind. Out went the hunter-gatherers and in came, about 6,000 years ago, the Neolithic farmers who hit on the bright idea of domesticating animals instead of chasing them all over the place. They also thought of tilling the ground and growing crops. They lived in communities and built cairns such as Gleamnach, to name but one of many – circular stone chambers which they covered with earth and in which they buried their dead.

We head up the Glen, following the route of the Old Military Road, the present A93, along the banks of the Black Water. Once upon a time, so legend says, there was a mad, wild boar on the rampage, roaming the glen killing both folks and livestock. King Fingal had a cunning plan, however. He ordered his right-hand man, Diarmid, to dispatch the boar. A handsome man was he, with mighty muscles – a bit of a medieval babe-magnet, in fact. Fingal's queen was Diarmid's number one fan: she was having an affair with him, which is how her husband's plan was so cunning. In happier times, Fingal and the queen had produced a son, Ossian, the poet, whom Macpherson "translated" as you will remember from Chapter Three. Fingal's plan, at the very least, put Diarmid at some distance from the queen and with a bit of luck, so he hoped, the boar might gore him.

Diarmid killed the boar and, as evidence, bore the head back to Fingal. Alas, he did not escape unscathed as Fingal

The Cockstane

saw to it that Diarmid was denied any treatment for his wounds and he died as a result. It was a hollow victory, however. Grief-stricken at the loss of her lover, the queen committed suicide.

Some say Diarmid was none other than Lancelot in Arthurian legend. Be that as it may, Clan Campbell claims him as their progenitor, and – hang on to your hat – that his mistress (or his mother) Queen Guinevere, was a local lass, born and bred in Blairgowrie. What happened to her in the end, you already know.

Andrew MacThomas of Finegand, 19th Chief of Clan MacThomas

Not far after the B951 junction to Cray but still on the A93, is a very remarkable boulder, a glacier erratic actually, called *Clach-na-Coileach* or "Cockstane". You can't see it from the road, but you will be alerted to it by a noticeboard on top of a bank by the roadside.

We pull into the small car park to find a car already there. As we are getting our things together we are hailed by a gentleman wearing gardening gloves and grasping a pair of long-handled shears. Presumably he had been alerted to our presence by the slamming of car doors and the sound of our voices. He introduces himself as Andrew MacThomas of Finegand, 19th Chief of Clan MacThomas. He is here with David Milanes to do a bit of tree maintenance. What a remarkable thing – to find a Chief still working the land which his forebears first settled over five hundred years ago!

Andrew leads us through a gate onto which the Chief's crest is affixed. It strikes me as being rather amusing. It features an astonished-looking wildcat holding a serpent (somewhat tenderly, it has to be said) by the throat. He really should be more alert. He hasn't noticed just how close that flickering forked tongue is to giving him a bite, and it won't be of the loving sort either.

The path to the stone is lined by snowberry bushes, the Clan plant. And while I am at it, let me tell you the Clan motto is *Deo juvante invidiam superabo*, which in case, like me, you have let your Latin slip a bit since you left school, means "With God's help, I shall overcome envy". I wish I had a motto like that. I feel quite jealous.

It's only a short walk to where the Cockstane sits in a natural amphitheatre like an egg in a nest. Attached to it there is a very interesting story indeed.

In 1635, so the story goes, the men of Atholl were collecting their dues, the rent, or for those who were unable to pay with hard cash – *kain* – payment in kind. There was a poor widow who was scraping a living from half-a-dozen chickens, for their eggs and, every so often, a sacrificial victim for the pot. She also had a rooster who made his own contribution to her livelihood, such as it was, by fathering more chickens. The taxmen, who were notorious for taking more than their due, didn't give a jot for the poor old woman's impoverishment and commandeered the lot, stuffed the live birds into a sack and left the old woman to her fate. Desperate, the *cailleach* appealed to the great McComie *Mor*, aka Iain Mor, 7th Chief of Clan MacThomas. Hastily, he assembled a handful of henchmen and they set off in pursuit of the heartless men of Atholl.

They caught up with them at the *Clach-na-Coileach* and demanded the return of the poultry. When they refused, Iain Mor, with a single, mighty blow of his claymore, separated the leader's head from his shoulders, then he and his men set about the rest. A moment later, three more of the Earl's men lay dead amongst the heather. Discretion became the better part of valour. The survivors fled for their lives, casting aside their weapons in their haste.

Meanwhile, the hens emerged from the sack and the cockerel, delighted to see the light of day again, flapped as far as his feeble wings would take him onto the top of the boulder. From this lofty perch, he crowed lustily to celebrate his and the hens' freedom. His celebration was short-lived, however. He and his common-law wives were recaptured, returned to the sack, and taken back to their rightful owner.

As for Iain Mor, he went on to achieve further deeds which made him a legend in his own lifetime. In response to the event above, and as a sort of bodyguard to his taxmen, the Earl of Atholl imported a champion swordsman from Italy. Iain Mor soon saw to that plan. He slew him in single combat. He also killed a man who had insulted his wife; fought his son in disguise to test his courage; and wrestled with and defeated, with his bare hands, a bull.

A plaque on the boulder divulges the information that this is also the spot where Clan MacThomas (from the Gaelic *MacThomaidh)* hold a gathering every three years amidst a great deal of pageantry and piping. The next one was scheduled to take place in August 2020, until the coronavirus pandemic put paid to it.

The origins of the Clan go back to the 15th century and *Thomaidh Mor*, or Big Tommy, of the Clan Chattan Mackintoshes in Badenoch. His great-grandfather was the 8th Chief of the Chattan Confederation. There is such a thing as being too successful in a land that is not fertile enough to sustain large numbers of people. Accordingly, Big Tommy led his kinsmen to pastures new. The promised land turned out to be Glenshee, centred around a spot on the eastern side of the Shee Water, opposite the present-day Spittal of Glenshee, and incidentally, the supposed burial place of Diarmid whose exploits we read about above.

After the 4th Chief MacThomas was oh, so foully murdered by caterans circa 1600, the Chiefdom passed to his brother, John McComie of nearby Finegand, and it has remained the seat of the Chiefs ever since. The name comes from the Gaelic *Fèith nan Ceann* meaning "burn of the heads". Not those, please note, which had formerly been attached to the shoulders of Atholl's tax collectors – this refers to an earlier decapitation event. A tax collector's lot is not a happy one, happy one, as Gilbert and Sullivan might have put it, and to this day you will never hear employees of HM Revenue and Customs bragging in the pub about what they do to earn a crust.

Mind you, it wasn't a barrel of laughs being a Clan Chief in the 17th century either. As often as not, the neighbours were troublesome, if not downright nasty. In 1606, about 200 caterans made up mainly of MacGregors, made off with about 2,700 of MacThomas cattle together with 100 of their horses. The clansmen caught up with the rustlers near the Devil's Elbow and defeated them at what came to be known as the "Battle of Cairnwell". It was a Pyrrhic victory, however. The MacGregors slaughtered most of the cattle. If they couldn't have them, then neither could the MacThomases. It spelled financial ruin for many of the families. Cattle was their livelihood, and there is only so much dead cow you can eat in the days before refrigeration.

Another dispute over cattle took place some seventy years later. It's another Iain Mor story, only this time things didn't go quite so well for him. The problem was the MacThomases were allowing their cattle to graze on Farquharson lands, though Iain Mor claimed he had bought them fair and square from Lord Airlie and they had every right to be there. It all came to a bloody conclusion in a skirmish at Drumgley, near Forfar, on 28th January 1673 where Iain Mor's son and heir, John, and his fourth son, Robert, were slain. That was bad, but more mis-

Highland Cows near Bridge of Cally

fortune was to follow. In the lawsuit that followed, the MacThomases were handed a crippling fine and, after Iain Mor's death in 1674, the surviving sons were forced to sell their lands.

And so it came to pass that the clan was dispersed, some going south to Tayside, some going north to Aberdeenshire, and to this day – rather sadly – there are very few kinsmen living in the ancient lands of their ancestors. After the death of Thomas, the 9th Chief, the title became dormant. Then came the great Highland romantic revival pioneered by Sir Walter Scott when he turned George IV's state visit to Scotland in 1822 into a celebration of all things Scottish. Even the king joined into the spirit of things, getting gussied up in Highland garb complete with salmon-pink tights. God forbid!

The board to which I referred earlier informs us there are fifteen variants of the name MacThomas, such as Thomson and Thom. It is easy to see that connection, but the likes of MacOmie and McOmish, McColm and McCombie are not quite so obvious. The fist pair are actually an Anglicised spelling of the Gaelic pronunciation of "Th", that is to say an "H" sound, while the second pair come from a transcription of the Gaelic letter τ, which, as you can see, looks rather like a "C". By Acts of the Scottish Parliament in 1587 and 1595, MacThomas became the official name of the clan.

In 1954, the Clan Society was founded with members in Norway, Sweden, Germany, Australia, USA and Canada, and as the plaque on the *Clach-na-Coileach* testifies, the land around the site where the boulder sits was purchased for the clan in 1969 by a member of the Chief's family. In the 1970s, Andrew, the 19th Chief, made the site over to the Clan Society in perpetuity and began restoring it to what it would have looked like in the days of his ancestors by planting rowans, cherries, hazel, birch, white beam – all of which already look pretty-well established. To the Scots pine and the oaks which were already flourishing on the site, he added more oaks.

As you can see, Andrew takes his duties as Chief extremely seriously. He negotiated with Tayside Council to have the new bridge at the Spittal named the "MacThomas Bridge". It opened in 1984. He has also been a tireless ambassador for the Clan, travelling to Australia, South Africa and Canada, not forgetting the USA which he has visited many, many times.

As JFK didn't quite say: "Ask not what your clan can do for you, but what you can do for your clan".

Chapter Seven

Finegand to the Glenshee Ski Centre: A "Grave" and the Devil's Elbow

SO it's farewell to the Chief and onwards and upwards through Glenshee towards Spittal. The name "Spittal" is supposed to come from *An Spideal*, meaning "a hospice" or "hospital". The snag is that no evidence of such a place has ever been discovered. The earliest reference is to "Spittale of Glensche" which was mentioned in the records in 1542. There may have been a chapel there by the beginning of the 17th century, and that is more or less the sum total of what we know about Spittal's past. It's more likely therefore that the word comes from a corruption of the Gaelic *pas cumhang eadar cnuc*, meaning "a narrow pass between hills". And if you're wondering, like me, how they get *spideal* from that, then I am at a loss too, but what I can say is that it fits the physical description of the place perfectly. And as Sherlock Holmes remarked, "when you have eliminated the impossible, whatever remains, however improbable, must be the truth".

Fans of going fast downhill on snow have been gravitating to Glenshee since 1950 when the Dundee Ski Club set up the first ski-tows in Britain. Their meeting place was the Spittal Hotel, which unfortunately burned down in 1959. Out of the ashes arose a new hotel. They say lightning doesn't strike twice, but nobody said anything about fires. Believe it or not, the hotel caught fire again in 2014.

No-one, so far, has had the courage to try re-building a third time, and frankly, I don't think I would either, though having the

Remains of the Spittal Hotel

money first would be a fine thing. I'm not a superstitious sort of person who believes that things, especially of the bad kind, happen in threes, but I am doubtful if it would be a sound investment. Despite what the deniers may say, global warming is an incontrovertible fact and one wonders just how much snow there may be on the ski slopes in the near-years to come. Skis may have to be exchanged for sun-loungers, sun-umbrellas and an open-air swimming pool, but I can't see Spittal competing with somewhere in Spain, somehow.

Spittal Parish Church

The site formerly occupied by the hotel looks like a bomb site. Through the metal fence we can see some stone walls still standing, a blackened fireplace, a green carpet of weeds, and most strikingly, a twisted girder, which tells you how intense the heat must have been. Rather bizarrely, an abandoned wheelchair sits on the tarmac looking as if it had just been left there after the occupant had been transferred to an ambulance and taken to hospital, although, as a matter of fact, mercifully, the hotel was unoccupied at the time of the conflagration.

It's not far from there to the Parish Church where, behind it on *Dun Sith* ("Hill of the Fairies"), there is a standing stone almost six foot high and over two foot wide. It is very much weathered, and they are pretty hard to make out, but if you wade through the knee-high grass, you might just be able to make out some crescent shapes about half-way up. As to what they mean, your guess is a good as mine. From there, and before the kirk got in the way, you would have been able to see the so-called "Four Poster" stone circle a little to the east on the other side of the *Allt a' Ghlinne Bhig*.

Actually, it isn't really a circle at all but where Diarmid of the last chapter is said to be buried after being killed by the boar. Interesting. According to this version, Fingal's cunning plan to get rid of his wife's lover for good was indeed successful without any need for his intervention. Others say it is the grave of *Diarmuid Ua Duibhne* of the *Fionn mac Cumhaill* sagas in Irish folklore. It's easy to see how the confusion could arise, but what the heck would the Irish Diarmuid have been doing in this neck of the woods?

The "grave" consists of four stones placed at each corner of the mound. Spoiler alert. In 1894, archaeologists drilled down to a depth of twenty feet and – surprise, surprise – found no signs of the bones of the mythical warrior, not

Old Bridge at Spittal

even a burial chamber. What the drilling *did* confirm, however, was that the mound was created by glaciation – a moraine, in fact. The ancients didn't know that, of course, and to their eyes it looked a special place which they marked by reverently placing the stones to delineate the place where they truly believed Diarmid was sleeping throughout eternity.

For a stone circle that is actually a square, the stones are pygmies, barely poking out of the long grass. The largest is two-and-a-half-feet high, the smallest, just under a foot. If you wish to visit the site you will find it at the bottom of *Bad an Loin,* just off the Cateran Trail. It's an added point of interest to a trail which offers spectacular views to the south-east along Glen Shee, and north-east towards the Grampians.

From the kirk, the road ahead lies over the Glen Lochsie Burn which is crossed by a humpback bridge. A helpful noticeboard nearby tells us it was built in 1749 at the cost of £40. You will not be surprised to learn it is part of the system attributed to General Wade. It also shows how they built this bridge and others, using a wooden framework called a "falsework".

It may be narrow and it may be old, and it was never designed to bear the weight of modern vehicles, but you can drive over it if you dare. We do dare. The bonnet of the car points to the sky and the road momentarily disappears. What if we meet another vehicle coming the other way? But we weren't quite as foolhardy as I have made it sound: a clear view can be seen if there is any oncoming traffic before you set off. It's with relief we see the road ahead again and shortly afterwards we rejoin the A93 as it follows the course of the *Allt a' Ghlinne Bhig.*

Onwards and upwards we go until we reach the first, or last, depending on your direction of travel, of three art installations. It's called "Connecting Contours" and

Connecting Contours **Art Installation**

The view from *Connecting Contours*

it's the brainchild of Daniel Smith and Philip Zoechbauer. As its name suggests, it has much to do with the contours of the hills as seen on an OS map. Plaques at the place show them in all their curvaceous seductiveness. It's a delight for geographers (like my companion) but for humbler mortals like myself, it's a just a joy to sit on one of the benches, gaze at, and admire the scenery, and look back down at the road we have just come and see it and the *Allt a' Ghlinne Bhig* snaking into the distance until they disappear from sight.

In the other direction, a mile south of the 2,199-foot Cairnwell Pass (the highest in the whole of the United Kingdom), is the infamous Devil's Elbow. It appears on Taylor and Skinner's map of 1776, by-passing the old military road built by Caulfeild. It was by-passed itself at the end of 1960s. *And so it goes*, as Billy Pilgrim said, many, many times in *Slaughterhouse-Five*.

Reports of the Elbow's steepness have been greatly exaggerated. In actual fact is is "only" a 1-in-6 gradient, a slope that struck fear into the motorists of yesteryear. The AA used to maintain a well in a lay-by for the relief of overheated engines, and bus passengers used to get out before the bends in order to lighten the load. I dare say some were very happy at this arrangement, secretly relieved that if the bus didn't make it, they were not on board as it careered backwards and not trusting to the brakes to stop it.

It's only a slight detour down an unpaved track to where you can park and walk to where the bends start. The road ahead, however, tarmac-clad, looks in a far better condition than the track we have just come down, despite having more potholes than a WWI battlefield. Being the driver, I make an executive decision to give the car park a miss and head towards the first bend of the Elbow where I reverse into a wide expanse of grass.

The Devil's Elbow

As I walk uphill towards

the second, steeper bend, I note tyre tracks left in the soft verge by a previous intrepid motorist. It is not so much the steepness, but the *narrowness* of the road that strikes me. The motorists of yesteryear could not have felt so confident as we were before we drove over the packhorse bridge at the Spittal, that their cars, already pushed to their limits, might meet another vehicle coming down at the crown of the blind bend. To have to stop and then do a hill start would be the severest test, not only of the handbrake, but the driver's clutch control.

A famous photograph taken in 1967 shows some people standing at the second bend and waving to the Queen, who is being driven in a Daimler by Prince Phillip. Of course he was a lot younger then and I am sure his driving skills at that time were something in which the Queen had an absolute trust. Furthermore, I wouldn't be surprised in the least to learn that the road ahead had already been closed to other motorists and Phillip knew he could negotiate the bends in the absolute certainty that he need not necessarily keep to his side of the road.

An older sepia photograph shows a bus negotiating the same bend and, sure enough, the passengers seem to have bailed out and are standing on the verge on the far side of the bus. It does indeed look as if it is having a great deal of difficulty. I can't help but think if the passengers hadn't bailed out, it would never have made it, and even now, whether or not it will, hangs in the balance. A bit of collective pushing, I'm sure, would have been much appreciated by the driver, if only his passengers had been brave enough to ignore the possibility that the bus might roll back on top of them.

In the distance, off to our left, it is a surprise to see some unsightly concrete blocks littering the hillside. They are WWII anti-tank cubes, the remains of a defence line called the "Cowie Line" that ran from here to Stonehaven. Its purpose was, in the event of a German invasion force landing on the north-eastern beaches, to prevent them advancing south. There used to be a pillbox behind the place where I parked the car, whose purpose was to guard the bend. Thankfully it was never needed, and was removed when the road was improved many years later.

Anti-Tank Installations near the Devil's Elbow

Onwards and upwards, we stop at the Glenshee Ski

Centre which, at 2,132 feet, sits in a bowl a little to the north of the Cairnwell Pass. It consists of, on the western side, Cairnwell (3,061 ft) and *Càrn Aosda* (meaning "aged hill" or "cairn", or even "Hill of the Inn"). The inn was the original hospital or place of refuge for travelers, from whence the village derived its name. The mountain just squeaks in as a Munro at 3,008 ft). On the eastern side is *Glas Maol* (3,503 ft

Glenshee Ski Centre

– meaning the "green lump"). Covering 25 miles of pistes overall, it is the UK's largest skiing destination. There are 3 chair lifts, 14 Pomas, 3 T-bar lifts and 1 rope tow to help you access 36 runs of various difficulty, including two black runs. They make it so easy for skiers nowadays.

At the other end of the skiing colour spectrum, there are orange runs for the kids and beginners, as well as a ski and snowboard school. There is more parking space than you can shake a ski pole at and if the hills don't already state the obvious, you get a real sense that you are in the Highlands, if not a foreign land, when you see the signs in Gaelic, as well as English, for the chair-lift tickets, ski-hire and not least, the toilets. But "accidents" at ground level surely are preventable, and bilingual signs to the toilets make sure that they are.

The chairlift operates in the summer as well as in winter, and – in exchange for a few coins of the realm – it will whisk you to the top of Cairnwell in far less time and huff and puff than if you elected to go by Shanks's Pony. At the top, if you have the time and inclination, there are a number of walks you can take where you can expect to meet some of the residents: red grouse, mountain hares and ptarmigan. As a bonus, if you are lucky, you might spot golden eagles and peregrine falcons, as well as other birds such as dotterel, golden plover, ring ouzels and the rare snow bunting. You might also come across the greater-spotted mountain biker because there is a twenty-mile bike track across the mountains, coded blue, with two uphill sections.

Having admired the stupendous views all around, you have the option of returning by chairlift or better, walking back down, which gives you the chance to admire the scenery for longer.

Ski-Lift at Glenshee Ski Centre

The Ski Centre is also a very good place if you would like to take up a new hobby of Munro-bagging, as the car park's lofty elevation gets you off to a flying start. Over a distance of 18 gently-sloping miles you can tick off no fewer than four peaks. Only 280 left to go. You can knock them off over a lifetime, but today you could just go for a ramble in the hills.

On the hillside opposite the ski centre there used to be a statue of an elderly couple, Tom and Maggie, sculpted by Malcolm Robertson in the 1970s. Old photos show Tom craning his neck to see the hills behind him to his right, while Maggie is shading her eyes against the sun and looking at something somewhere off to her left. It seems to me as if they may be having a domestic – perhaps about what she sees as his enthusiastic efforts to prop up the Scottish economy by drinking the distilleries dry, whereas he says he only takes the *uisgue-beatha* for the good of his health.

Alas, they are no more. They fell foul of the snow, which took them into that "undiscover'd country from whose bourn no traveller returns", as Hamlet told us.

Chapter Eight

Braemar: A Castle, a Saint, a Teller of Tales and Two Memorials

DESPITE sounding like somewhere in Italy, at Braemar's back door, so to speak – Morrone (2,815 feet) – is an easy ascent (so I am told). I can believe it, as you are already at an elevation of 1,112 feet before you start off. It falls short of being a Munro (over 3,000 feet) but it is both a Corbett (between 2,500 and 3,000 feet) and a Marilyn (over 492 feet) – a strange height to settle on until you translate it into metric and you find it works out at 150 metres. The name was wittily coined by Alan Dawson in his *Relative Hills of Britain* (1992).

I need scarcely point out that Sir Hugh Munro (1856-1919), who mapped the mountains which were named after him, is no relative in any shape or form of Marilyn Monroe (1926-62), aka Norma Jeane Mortenson or Baker – but I can see, apart from the alternative spelling of the surname, where Mr Dawson got the idea from. As regards "Morrone", no-one is sure where that name comes from, but it means "Big Nose".

The name "Braemar" comes from the Gaelic *Bràigh Mhàrr*, literally "the upper part of Marr" – that is to say the area west of Aboyne. Lying at the confluence of the Clunie Water and the River Dee, it only adopted that name after 1870, but its origins go back to the 11th century when there were two hamlets on either side of the Clunie Water: *Baile a' Chaisteil* or Castleton on the east, and *Ach an Droighinn* or Auchendryne, meaning "thorn field", on the west. Malcolm III is said to have built a wooden bridge to link the two settlements and a wooden castle to defend them. It was called *Cinn Drochaid* (Kindrochit in English), meaning "bridge end". Nothing of that remains now, not surprisingly, but we know from charters that he issued from there that it was occupied by Robert II between 1371 and 1388 when he came on annual hunting expeditions.

The stone ruins that you see today date from the late 14th century, when Robert III granted his brother-in-law Sir Malcolm Drummond, Earl of Mar, permission to "build a tower or fortalice on the lands of Kyndrocht". One should always choose one's brothers-in-law carefully. Alas for Drummond, the royal connection was a bit of a poisoned chalice. Before the building was completed, he was murdered round about 1402 by Alexander Stewart, son of the notorious Wolf of Badenoch who, in 1390, famously and unforgivably, put Elgin to the torch, sparing neither the town, Greyfriars monastery, nor the cathedral.

It is a truth universally acknowledged that a widow in possession of a large fortune must be sought after by would-be husbands in pursuit of money and status. Not satisfied with the murder of Drummond, the Wolf's equally ruthless cub attacked Kildrummy Castle, the seat of the Earls of Mar. He may, or may not, have had admired the lady, but reader, he forced her to marry him and thus in 1404, became the Earl of Mar and all that that entailed – her lands and money, *jure uxoris,* by right of his wife. (Incidentally, and incredible but true, it was not until 1881 that women in Scotland were allowed to keep their property after marriage. England cottoned on a year later.)

She was Lady Isabella Douglas who was elevated to the Countess of Mar when her brother, James 2nd Earl of Douglas, fell at the Battle of Otterburn in 1388 as he was leading the Scots to victory over Henry "Hotspur" Percy. Her new spouse had the ear of the Duke of Albany, the younger brother and regent for Robert III who, as well as being a weak ruler, was also a weak man, especially after his horse kicked him in the sorest place of all. As for Isabella, she died childless in 1408. Hopefully, Stewart did not press his entitlement to marital rights; he was only interested in the title and the money.

Dirty deeds of another sort happened two centuries later. Legend has it that at the beginning of the 17th century, the inhabitants of the castle fell victim to a plague and it was blown up by cannon fire with them still inside, in order to prevent the pestilence from spreading. Whatever the truth of that may be, the castle certainly lay in ruins by 1618.

Noticeboards which are dotted throughout the site help you interpret the ruins, which are free to enter. An artist's impression shows what it might have looked like in the 15th century. It was drawn by the archaeologist who excavated the castle in the 1920s, Dr W. Douglas Simpson. He was no mean artist, and very impressive the castle looks with its towers and castellations and a wooden barri-

Detail from Kindrochit Castle

Inside Kindrochit Castle

cade running round the outer courtyard.

The walls of the pit prison are ten feet thick and not all of the castle walls are as impressively thick as that but, even so, the castle must have presented a bit of a challenge to those who reduced it to rubble on top of the heads of the plague victims – if they did.

Another story goes that in 1746 a Redcoat was lowered into one of the vaults in search of buried treasure. To his horror, what he saw there was a ghostly company seated around a table piled high with human skulls. He must have thought he had descended into hell and either had consumed some sort of substance or had a very vivid imagination. This we know to be the case, because when Dr Simpson conducted his excavations, he found no such skulls, nor any remains of the plague victims. But what a troop of Boy Scouts, working under his supervision, *did* find in the pit prison was treasure in the form of a rather splendid silver-gilt brooch dating from the late 15th century. I bet, despite their motto, they were not prepared for that.

The brooch is now in the safe-keeping of the National Museum of Scotland. For the benefit of visitors, a sculpture in stone – many times life-size – can be seen on the site. Scallop-shaped, an inscription in Gothic lettering in bad French runs round it which reads: *Ani io cne ab an hi.* It means "I am in place of a friend". I can imagine the lady owner clasping it and getting some comfort from that. But who she was, and why was she imprisoned there, we do not know. And why is the inscription not in very good French? The frustrating truth is it seems unlikely that these questions will ever be answered.

Human remains were not found, thankfully, but bones of a different kind were discovered in the kitchen area. Along with those you might expect – ox, sheep, pig, deer and salmon – they also found those of horse, otter, fox and even an eagle. No comment.

And whilst on the subject of bones, it is said that those of St Andrew, who died in AD60 in Patras, Greece, rested in Braemar on their way to their final resting place in St Andrews. It never ceases to intrigue me how, after they have shuffled off the mortal coil, saints' bodies have a tendency to be chopped up and splattered all around the globe. So, how did Andrew's get from Greece to Scotland, you might well ask?

One version is that Rule, later St Regulus – the monk who had custody of the bones – was told in a dream to hide some of them and wait for further instructions. Shortly afterwards, in 324AD, the Emperor Constantine, the first Roman Christian Emperor, seized what was left of the remains and whisked them off to Constantinople, formerly Byzantium, the new hub of the Roman Empire and which he modestly named after himself. Then the angel came again unto Rule and told him to take ship and sail as far west as he could until he was shipwrecked and, wherever that turned out to be, he was to found a church in Andrew's name. Poor Rule! What sort of a mission is that? Undertaking a voyage in those days was perilous enough, but it must have been something worse to be sure it was destined to end badly.

He set off on his ill-fated journey in 345AD and eventually was driven ashore off the headland of Muckross in Fife where there was a village called Kilroymont. But what has all that got to do with Braemar, you might rightly ask? Well, an alternative version of the story goes that it was not Rule, but Bishop Acca of Hexham who picked up St Andrew's bones while he was on his second tour of Rome in 690. For reasons that are not entirely certain, he fled his see in 732AD, taking the bones with him. He showed them to Óengus I, King of Picts (732-761). His seat was called "Doldencha", built to guard the ford, pretty close to where the present castle of Braemar stands today. And that is how St Andrew's bones came to Braemar. A rickle of bones does not a body make, and there are many conflicting stories about the Bishop's movements after he left Hexham (to say nothing of Andrew's bones), but if the good citizens of Braemar like to believe the saint's body rested here, who am I to disappoint them?

And talking of stories, one of the greatest teller of tales the world has ever known once stayed here on holiday. He was known by the natives of Samoa as *Tusitala* which means "Teller of Tales", but to his family he was known as Robert Louis Stevenson and it was for his 12-year-old stepson, Lloyd, that when the weather was wet and dreary, RLS wrote the first fifteen chapters of that classic of children's literature – *Treasure Island,* though it was called *The Sea Cook* at that time. Well done that editor for changing the title!

Holiday home of Robert Louis Stevenson

The house, at 3 Glenshee Road, is a two-storey granite affair just a stone's throw from Kindrochit Castle. A plaque above the door states:

HERE
R. L. STEVENSON
SPENT THE SUMMER OF 1881
AND WROTE "TREASURE ISLAND"
HIS FIRST GREAT WORK.

Some summer, some book! Some characters are said to be based on a number of the residents. You can believe that if you like, but it sounds like another case of St Andrew's bones to me.

Just stop a moment and reflect – but for that miserable weather, the book that inspired boys the world over to take up reading may never have been written, though it no longer casts the spell it once did. The present generation has moved on to tales of another sort.

While on the subject of bad weather, on 10th January 1982, a temperature of -27.2C was recorded in Braemar, equaling the record set by Altnaharra in Sutherland on 30th December 1895. It sounds more impressive translated into Fahrenheit -16.96 (that's nearly fifty degrees of frost) – cold enough, not so much to shiver your timbers, but turn your blood to ice.

The winter of 1942 was pretty bad too, and responsible for a tragedy. On 19th January 1942, Wellington Bomber R1644 set out from its base at RAF Lossiemouth on a routine training mission and crashed into a hillside near here. It was presumed lost at sea until about a month after its disappearance, a gamekeeper on the Invercauld estate, on the lookout for deer, saw through his binoculars something strange sticking out of the snow. The following morning, and although the snow was deep and the frost was cruel, a search party set out to investigate.

What they found was the tail-end of the plane and rear gun-turret poking out from beneath the snow. It took two months in very difficult circumstances to recover the bodies of the

Robert Louis Stevenson commemorative plaque

eight crew who came from three corners of the earth – England, Canada, Australia and New Zealand. Two of them were old men aged 29 and 25. The rest were aged between 19 and 23. Six were buried in Dyce Old Churchyard near Aberdeen; the remaining two were repatriated.

One of those who made up the original search party was the fifteen year-old Andy Brown. Andy had a dream that one day the aircrew and others who sacrificed their lives over the Cairgorms during the war should be remembered in a memorial. His dream finally began to take shape when in 1999, after a lot of effort by a lot of people, and not least a Sea King helicopter from Lossiemouth (appropriately enough), which effortlessly airlifted the two Pegasus engines from the crash site. The least damaged one was mounted on a plinth next to the war memorials in the town. Painted black and looking like some sort of malformed starfish, there is, rather fittingly, one propellor for each dead airman. A thing of beauty it most certainly is not, but that is rather fitting too in that it reflects the horror of war.

RAF Benevolent Fund Piggy Bank

It was unveiled on 21st August 2003 by the Princess Royal, and Andy's dream was finally fully realised in 2009 when RAF Lossiemouth donated a decommissioned practice bomb which was converted into a sort of enormous piggy bank to receive donations for the RAF Benevolent Fund. Painted a sinister shiny black, its nose firmly planted in concrete and its tail bristling with fins, it looks rather malevolent despite its purpose to the complete contrary.

You will find it opposite the Fife Arms Hotel, a former Victorian coaching inn and which was pressed into service in 1940 as barracks for the newly-formed commandos who were being trained in the art of mountain warfare in the hills hereabout. Meanwhile, the Invercauld Arms Hotel – which you will pass on the way to Braemar's other castle – served as a home for Belgian refugees, many of them children. Embedded in a standing stone opposite the hotel, there is a plaque with a most interesting inscription. It reads:

Erected by
the Deeside Field Club
in 1953, the Coronation year

of
ELIZABETH, QUEEN OF SCOTS,
to commemorate the
raising of the standard
on
6th September 1715 by
John Erskine, Earl of Mar.

It goes on to say there is another plaque inside the hotel which marks the spot where the standard was raised. (How do they know?) Then this: *Add Glory to the Past.*

I shall come back to the Earl of Mar later but, in the meantime, it needs to be noted and scarcely needs saying, that the Rising ended not in glory but in failure. Curious too, the Field Club's styling of the Queen. It makes me wonder if they considered adding the figure I after "Elizabeth" since of course, in all of Scotland's long history, there had never been a Queen Elizabeth before and so how could there be an Elizabeth II?

Chapter Nine

Braemar: Games, Gatherings, a Lodge and a Gorge

BRAEMAR'S royal connections are well known, as is its annual Gathering which really took off when Queen Victoria attended the event in 1848. It has, however, an ancient pedigree going all the way back to Malcolm III (reigned 1058-93), who came here and awarded prizes for feats of strength and skill including a race up *Creag Choinnich* (Kenneth's Hill) which is named after Kenneth II, who paid a visit earlier. Malcolm was known as "Canmore" or *ceann mòr* in the Gaelic, meaning "big head" or possibly "great leader". His father was Duncan, who was murdered in his bed by Macbeth in the eponymous play by Shakespeare. The events in the play, however, have only a nodding acquaintance with historical fact. The things that you're liable to see in the theatre, they ain't necessarily so.

After the unsuccessful Second Jacobite Rebellion of 1745, a raft of punitive measures were put in place to curb Highland culture but, as I said above, after Queen Victoria's visit, the Braemar Gathering was given an enormous boost. The spectacle takes place on the first weekend in September, so should you wish to witness it, you know when to come.

There are Highland games all over the world now, each with their own individual refinements, and you can find out all you need to know about them – and more particularly, the history of the Gatherings here, as well as its royal connections – in the Duke of Rothesay Highland Games Pavilion. It was formally opened by the Queen in 2018 and with its red roofs, pale green walls and white-

The Duke of Rothesay Pavilion, Braemar

Games Arena at Braemar

framed window panes, it's a very elegant, very English-looking building. This style is echoed in the buildings gathered around the games area, including the royal box. As most people know, the Duke of Rothesay is the Prince of Wales' Scottish title, but what most people probably don't realise is that the Pavilion is the first of the "7 for 70" projects to mark the Prince's 70th birthday and it's the only one to be located in Scotland.

Across from the car park and attached to the outside of the arena, huge photographs of the Games, past and present, give a flavour of what they are about. One particularly vivid action-shot shows a couple of men, kilt-clad, engaged in a wrestling match. Fortunately, neither is a true Scotsman, for both kilts are flaring high above waist level – and thus, mercifully, Her Majesty (and everyone else) is spared seeing rather more of her subjects than she would ever care to.

Arguably, the most interesting competitions are the so-called "heavy" events involving muscle-straining feats such as Throwing the Hammer, Putting the Stone and the world-famous Tossing the Caber.

The Hammer competition consists of throwing a cast-iron ball, jammed into a wooden shaft, where, one hopes, it remains stuck and does not fly off at a tangent to randomly land somewhere other than intended. There is a "light" hammer weighing 16lbs and a heavy one of 22lbs. But it's not what is thrown that impresses me so much as the iron spikes bolted onto the soles of the contestants' boots. They stick out a good foot from the toe. Anywhere outside this arena, they would be considered as offensive weapons – bovver boots intended to create grievous bodily harm.

The hammer-thrower, of course, has no intention of harming anyone. He needs to be firmly rooted to the spot so that, from a static position, he can swing the hammer round his waist three or four times before releasing it to land as far away as superhumanly possible and hopefully not on the napper of any of the unsuspecting judges who are patrolling the arena in the course of their duties. If you are a spectator, worry ye not about missiles going astray, for you are safely removed out of harm's way, just as the spectators in the amphitheatres of ancient Rome were when they witnessed spectacles of a much more bloody sort.

Not much needs to be said about Putting the Stone as it is similar to Putting the Shot in modern athletics. Like the Hammer event, there are two weights, 16lbs and 22lbs, and the "stone" is actually an iron ball. The contestant tucks the ball under his chin and with one hand, chucks it as far as he possibly can. He is allowed to run a maximum of 7 feet 6 inches before he reaches the throwing point, or "trig".

As for Tossing the Caber, there are two events at Braemar – the "Open" caber and the Braemar caber where entry to the latter is only available to those who have been successful in the first. The Open caber weighs 122lbs and is 19ft 9ins long; the Braemar version weighs 130lbs and is 20 feet 1 inch long. (I wonder who decided on that precise measurement?) And incidentally, the aim is not to see how far you can throw the mighty pole, but how close to the vertical you can toss it, base over apex.

Another heavy event is Throwing the Weight for Height. Here the object is to toss a 42lb or 56lb weight over a bar. It has a ring attached to it like that at the end of the piggy-wig's nose in *The Owl and the Pussycat*. Each competitor is given three attempts, and the bar is raised after each round. A photo shows a suitably-kilted contestant in action. Assuming him to be six feet tall (which is probably an underestimation), the bar must be fifteen feet high if it's an inch. He does well to keep his eye on it as it soars over the bar, as if it it would give him the mother of all headaches if it landed on the top of his dome. For your information, the record for the 56lb weight is 16ft 8ins which was set by K. Chupryne in 2005.

Throwing the Weight for Distance, as the name implies, involves throwing the weight as far as possible, only this time the weight has a short chain attached. There are two weights, the poncy 28lb lightweight and for real men, the 56lb job. Here, the competitor stands nine feet back from the release point and spins round like a dervish three times before launching it into the air.

Two more extraordinary spectacles are the Tug of War and Medley Relay for the armed services. The former involves twelve teams with eight pullers. They are divided into two groups, the top two of each group go through to the semi-finals and thence to the final where the Queen presents the trophy to the winning team. In addition to that, the individual members of both teams are presented with a highly-prized souvenir tankard.

As for the Medley Relay, there are ten teams of five individuals who can be either all male or all female or a mixture of both. Now, that's taking gender equality seriously! The first runner does half a lap, the second and third runners, a full lap, and the last runner, half a lap. And as with the Tug of War, the Queen presents the trophy to the winner and there are also tankard trophies for each competitor to put on their mantlepiece.

In addition to these attractions, there are track events and a sprint up Morrone and back for those who are so inclined. Hours of fun for all the family who sit on their *bahaookies* and the only sweat that dampens their brows is when the sun gets too hot (despite the RLS experience) as they watch the athletes bust a gut. That seems to me entirely the right way to look at the universe and reminds me very much of Jerome K. Jerome's (what a wonderful name!) immortal words in *Three Men in a Boat*: "I like work: it fascinates me. I can sit and look at it for hours".

Morrone from the Arena

And if all that were not enough, there are masses of kilts in all their infinite variety to be seen – a truly magnificent sight. And then there are piping competitions – piping, of course, being an integral part of Highland culture. Historically speaking, the pipes have accompanied men to war – to keep their spirits up; to strike fear into the enemy; and as as a lament for those who had lost their lives in battle. In Braemar, entry to the competition is restricted to thirty hopefuls who are judged on their appearance as well as their performance.

And where there is music, there shall be dancing. Nowadays, most of the competitive dancers are female, but it in the days of old, dancing was a serious business and done mainly by men. The Sword Dance, for instance, was yet another method by which the chiefs could determine who were the fittest and best suited to bear arms when it came down to a fight with the neighbours from hell, probably over the perennial problem of cattle and grazing rights.

The Sword Dance has another long pedigree. One legend pertaining to its origins is that in 1054, after killing one of Macbeth's generals, Malcolm Canmore placed his sword on top of that of his enemy and did a little victory jig over them. That may taken with a pinch of salt. More reliably, the first recorded instance of such a dance goes back to a "war dance" which was done to the skirl of the pipes at the nuptials of Alexander III's marriage to Margaret, daughter of Henry III of England, in 1251. She was eleven. He was ten. Ye gods!

The Highland Fling is another victory dance, supposedly. Because it is performed in a very small area, it is thought it would originally have been performed on top of the victor's shield, or targe. As anyone who has ever seen the dance knows very well, in addition to the deft movements of the feet, it involves a great deal of arm movements and is said to suggest the shape of a deer's antlers, an animal much admired by the Highlanders for its speed and agility.

As we all know, dancing is sinful, and the Calvinists did their best to suppress it in the 16th century. I wish they had been around when I was a lad, as it would have meant I would have avoided the dreaded Scottish Country dancing lessons. Whilst my friends were free to indulge in boyish pursuits such as building a hut in the woods, I was cooped up in the school having to dance with *girls!* In the end, I moaned so much about this loss of liberty, I was finally released with the caveat that I would live to regret it. I never have.

Another respite for those who hate the dance came in the 18th century when the 1746 Act of Proscription banned all things pertaining to Highland culture, including dancing – which just goes to show you that the Hanoverians weren't all bad. But then along came Sir Walter Scott and his Highland revival. (He knew not what he did to me.)

There are a good number of photographs in the Pavilion (including one of Queen Victoria in her widow's weeds looking very unamused), and so many silver trophies that your eyes are dazzled. There are other artefacts besides, too numerous to mention, but I must tell you about the Invercauld Stane which is tucked into a window alcove, along with a notice saying "Heavy object please do not attempt to lift". It seems a trifle superfluous, like warning people not to put their hand in a fire because it is hot. The notice goes on to say that stones like these were used by the chiefs to test a young man's strength. I would have thought if this boulder was a representative sample, the chiefs would have ended up with a bunch of men with hernias and much good that would have done them.

Robertson and Brown's 1843 *The New Guide to Deeside,* tells us the stone was called the "Erskine Stane" or "Muckle Stane o' the Clunie", and it was one of the markers to delineate the boundary between the Erskines of Clunie and the Farquharsons of Invercauld. And a fat lot the cattle cared about that in their never-ending quest for the sweetest grass, ironically not realising that the more they ate, the fatter they got and the sooner their date with a dinner plate.

Linn o' Dee

But for my money (and you don't need much of it), the best thing in the entire Pavilion is the octagonal lantern ceiling around which are grouped eight Highlanders in full regalia – and looking very splendid indeed. In actual fact, they are larger-than-life-size reproductions of watercolours by

Bridge to Mar Lodge

Kenneth Macleay RSA. A panel at eye level identifies them and their tartans. There are another twenty-thee portraits contained in two large leather-bound volumes *Highlanders of Scotland (1870)*. Should you wish to see them, you will need to ask the Queen very nicely. The originals form part of the Royal Collection at Windsor Castle.

As we leave the Pavilion, a brown sign says it is only six miles from here to the Linn o' Dee, and this is a beauty spot I have to see. It was one of Queen Victoria's favourite haunts and if it's good enough for her, then it is certainly good enough for me.

The river is narrow and the valley is wide. You can see it spread out before you from a lay-by which has ample parking. My ex-geography teacher of a wife (and much else besides) informs me that this is what people of her ilk call a "braided river" where the glacier has carved out a U-shaped valley (as opposed to a V-shaped one), leaving the poor little river acres of space to meander about in search of the unsighted sea.

A little further on we come to a suspension bridge, which, as the horseshoe arch over it tells us, is named after Queen Victoria. The other side tells us it was opened by Edward VII in 1905. It leads to the Mar Lodge, but not alas, for us, as there is a dirty big sign across the road saying "Road Closed". Not to worry; perhaps we can approach it from the other side of the river when we cross it at the Linn.

The Lodge is now in the care of the National Trust for Scotland but it was originally built in 1895 by Alexander Duff, 1st Duke of Fife (1849-1912), replacing an earlier building built in the 18th century by his ancestor, William Duff, Lord Braco. It was damaged beyond repair in the *Muckle Spate* or Great Flood of 1829, which devastated much of Strathspey. The event is described in an extremely long poem, divided into three *fyttes,* written in the Doric by David Grant in 1850. In some places the Dee rose an amazing 15 feet above its normal level but the worst-affected was Banchory where it rose an incredible 27 feet.

The Lodge was rebuilt, but it was destroyed by fire on 14th June 1895. If it's not one damned pestilence it's another. Victoria laid the foundation stone of the new building on 15th October of the same year. It was built in the Elizabethan style by architect Alexander Marshall MacKenzie of Aberdeen by the express wish of the Duchess of Fife who happened to be none other than the Princess Royal, Louise, the third child and eldest daughter of the future Edward VII. It's complicated, but she and her husband were third cousins who could both trace their ancestry from George III. On their marriage in 1895, the Queen elevated the groom to the dukedom and, while she was at it, also made him the Marquess of Macduff – which to my ear has fine ring to it.

The Duke had a very interesting death. In 1911, en route for Egypt aboard the SS *Delhi*, he and his family were shipwrecked. After spending some time in the water, they were eventually rescued but then had to face a trek through the desert before they found any accommodation.

Sadly, the Duke died of pleurisy the following month at Aswan, thought to be a result of the ordeal. His body was shipped home in a lead coffin and buried in St George's Chapel, Windsor. He did not rest easily in his grave, however. Five months later, he was uprooted and transferred to St Ninian's Chapel at Mar Lodge, and that is where he sleeps the Big Sleep to this very day.

By the way, the chapel was built at the same time as the Lodge, and you might care to know that the total cost for the lodge, stables and chapel came to £38,661, 13s, 1d. It seems funny money today, but what I find funniest of all is wondering what the penny was spent on. I suppose it was on one of the toilets, but when you are spending the best part of £40 grand on building a grand lodge, you might have thought they would have let you off the penny.

During his lifetime, the Duke was a bit of a party animal. It was said that more royal guests visited Mar Lodge than any other stately home, mansion, or castle in Scotland. They were relations, of course, but how terribly convenient to have one who had a place in the country where you could hoick salmon out of the river and shoot deer to your heart's content.

The lodge was completed in 1898 and, would you believe it, when it was being renovated in 1991, it caught fire once again and was extensively damaged. If you recall the fate of the hotel at the Spittal, it's yet another example of things happening in threes. Almost enough to turn you into a believer.

In 1995, as I said above, the lodge was taken over by the NTS and turned into self-catering holiday accommodation. A main feature of the property is the stag ballroom, which has precisely 2,435 stags' heads "adorning" the walls and ceiling. These are the trophies of the posh guests aforesaid. I, for one, really don't understand how they get a thrill out of the kill. I don't understand the joy of the dance either, as you know, but at least the only killing there should be to the feet of the dancers after a particularly gruelling session on the floor. Unlike the poor, defenceless deer, I have no sympathy for the dancers: I see sore feet as a self-inflicted injury. And surely, with all those dead heads staring glassy-eyed down on the dancers, any dances they perform should surely be of the macabre sort.

It's only a little further on to the Linn o' Dee where the river, flowing placidly along, minding its own business, suddenly, to its immense surprise, finds itself pinched into a narrow canyon where it undergoes a complete change of character. No Mister Nice Guy now but a raging brown torrent, a foaming angry mass of water, hell-bent on overcoming this unforeseen obstacle which seems to have been put in

River Dee

its path to thwart its destiny in the sea. If you wish to imagine the scene more precisely, may I refer you to Robert Southey's poem *The Cataract at Lidore*. For "Lidore", read "Linn of Dee". He describes it precisely, putting it so much more eloquently than I ever could.

While the Dee successfully overcomes its obstacle, once again we are thwarted in achieving our goal. The alternative access to Mar Lodge, along the north side of the river, is also closed. Some things are not meant to be.

Chapter Ten

Braemar Castle: Bobbing John, the Black Colonel and La Belle Rebelle

NOW we are making our way out of Braemar towards Balmoral where the town's other castle sits on a grassy hillock. With its round turrets and castellations, it looks very much like something out of a fairytale. It was built in 1628 by the 19th Earl of Mar (1558-1634) as a hunting lodge and also as defence against the nasty neighbours, their vassals actually, the Farquharsons of Inverey whose lands were a little to the east. It occupied a strategic location controlling access through Glen Derry to the north and Glen Clunie to the south. It was a five-storey L-shaped tower house with a walled courtyard or *barmkin* where the bakery, kitchens and stables would have been.

In March 1567, Mary, Queen of Scots had entrusted her nine-month old son, James, to be "conserved, nursed and upbrought" by the 18th Earl of Mar and the Countess at Stirling Castle. As the boy king grew up, Stirling became the centre for the Protestant faction while his mother's Catholic supporters were based in Edinburgh. The future 19th Earl was only a few years older than James and he was entrusted with being his guardian. Some guardian! He was to become one of the Ruthven Raid conspirators, a plot to distance James further from the French (and Catholic) influence and to prevent Mary, ex-Queen of Scots', return from England.

James was seized in August 1582 while hunting near Ruthven Castle (renamed "Huntingtower" after 1600) and held captive for nearly a year in the conspirators' houses, being passed from one to the other like a parcel. He was finally given his freedom in July 1583. Mar thought it politic to put some distance between him and his old pal for a while and fled to England, where he received the protection of Elizabeth I who tried to intercede on his behalf. It was unsuccessful and, in 1585, Mar and his friends returned to Stirling with an army, not bent on regime change, but to make their peace with the King.

By this time, James was nearly twenty and becoming more independent. He accepted Mar's pledge of loyalty, who then went on to make a meteoric rise to favour. He was appointed governor of Edinburgh Castle and tutor to James's son, Henry. That shows a great deal of trust, does it not? Not only that, but his lands, including the family seat at Kildrummy, were restored to him after having been held by the Crown since 1426.

You can see just how close he was to the King from this transcript of a letter dated 18th May 1607 which is on display in the castle. It reads as follows:

> *DEAR JOCK – As I'm going to give an audience this morning to the French Ambassador, I desire you to be sae gude as tae send me a pair of your best silken hose, with the goud clocks at them.*
> *Your affectionate Cousin,*
> *James R*

The next significant event in the castle's history occurred after the "Glorious Revolution" of 1688, which replaced James II (or VII) with the Protestant William and Mary. The following year, John Farquharson of Inverey attacked and defeated a detachment of government dragoons on their way to protect the castle and put it to the torch. He was known as the "Black Colonel"; black because of his swarthy complexion, and colonel because he was given that rank by his leader, John Graham of Claverhouse, aka "Bonnie Dundee". But he might just as well have been called "black" for his misdeeds. In 1666, he had been outlawed for murder.

He took part in the Battles of Bothwell Bridge (1667) and Killiecrankie (1689) and survived that conflict, unlike Claverhouse. He was a larger-than-life sort of character whose deeds have passed into folklore. Apparently his preferred method of summoning a servant was to fire a pistol. History does not record what the lady of the house thought of that, but I imagine she was not best pleased at the damage being done to the decor. On one occasion, he escaped being captured by the dragoons by riding up the precipitous north side of the Pass of Ballater. *In*

Braemar Castle

extremis, needs must. He made another narrow escape when he was forewarned that the dragoons were lying in wait for him. He watched from a safe distance as his castle went up in flames. What goes around, comes around.

Homeless, he found refuge beneath a rocky overhang in a gorge in the River Ey (pronounced *eye*). His faithful mistress, Annie *Ban* or Annie the Fair, brought him food and other comforts. The place came to be known as the "Colonel's Bed". As it happens, he did not have much longer to live. He died in 1705, and his dying wish was to be buried at Inverey with Annie.

He was married twice, both times to Margarets, as it happens, and since we do not know when they died, perhaps his wish to be buried with Annie was an attempt to dodge the vexed question of which wife he should chose to sleep with throughout eternity. Whatever the truth of the matter, his request was ignored. They interred him at Braemar – or at least tried to. The morning after the burial, his coffin was found lying beside his empty grave. They reburied it, only for the same thing to happen again. When it happened yet a third time, they took the coffin to Inverey and buried him there. And there he stayed put. Home at last, and he could rest in peace.

The castle that the Black Colonel burnt remained in ruins for the next sixty years and the estates regained by the 19th Earl, as I explained above, were lost by his descendant, John Erskine (1675-1732), aka the 23rd Earl, or the 11th, or the 6th, depending where you start counting. Like some people's lives, it is complicated, and I will not weary you with too many details, but basically if the lands and titles became attainted or forfeited (as they often were for acts against the Crown), when they were reassigned at the discretion of the monarch, this new "creation" – as it was called – might continue where it left off, or might start again "from the very beginning", like Maria sang in *The Sound of Music*.

I'll call him the 23rd Earl. He was a key proponent of, and player in, negotiating the Act of Union of 1707, but he later made an amazing *volte face* by leading the Rising of 1715. He had had a glittering career under Queen Anne (ruled 1702-14), serving twice as Secretary of State for Scotland, as Keeper of the Signet, as a Privy Counsellor and, after 1707, a Representative Peer in the House of Lords. During his time there, he had a reputation for sometimes supporting the Tories, sometimes the Whigs, whatever suited him best, and thus earning the disrespect of all. For this reason he was given the soubriquet *Bobbing John* or *Bobbin' Jock*.

By 1713, he had become disillusioned with the Act of Union. The catalyst for this was the imposition of a Malt Tax on Scotland which would severely dent the whisky industry and which Scotland could ill afford to pay anyway, being the poorer partner in this marriage of countries. Mar petitioned the Queen, pointing this out to her, but she refused to intervene. The Bill had already passed through the Commons, and so opponents of the Tax played their last card. On 1st June, in the House of Lords, the Earl of Seafield proposed that the Act of Union be dissolved. It lost by a mere four votes. The hated Malt Tax was passed into law on the 10th June 1713. I suspect not a lot of people today realise just how close the Union came to being dissolved so soon after its creation.

Despite his campaign against that hated tax and support for Dissolution of the Union, when George I arrived to occupy the vacant throne, as Third Secretary of State for Great Britain, Mar, forever bobbing, sent him an obsequious letter of welcome. He was wasting his time and his ink. The new king's posterior had hardly started warming the throne before he sacked Mar and a lot of other Tories besides.

Mar didn't take his dismissal too kindly, as people with big egos don't, and George I was just about to find out that he had made a very bad enemy indeed. Returning to Braemar, Mar raised a standard for King James VII where the Invercauld Arms now stands, as I mentioned earlier. The date was 6th September 1715, a day almost as famous in Scottish history as 23rd June 1314. In what some saw as a bad omen, the gilt ball at the top of the flagpole unaccountably detached itself and fell to the ground like a decapitated head.

Before too long, more that 10,000 men had rallied to the cause and, to begin with, it went very well indeed with Inverness, Aberdeen and Dundee falling to the rebels. A mere month after the standard was raised, Mar controlled the North. The trouble was that he whom they wanted to place on the throne was still in France. Nor did they liaise with Jacobite sympathisers in England. To be fair, such a thing was not so easily done in those days.

The bubble burst on 13th November 1715 at the Battle of Sheriffmuir, just to the north of Dunblane, where Mar's numerically superior men, marching south from Perth, encountered the Government troops led by John Campbell, 2nd Duke of Argyll. It was a draw in footballing terms, but for the Jacobites it meant the cause was lost. They retreated to Perth and holed up there.

While all this was going on, there was, co-incidentally, a simultaneous event happening at Preston. It was not dignified with the name of "battle", but called the "Fight of Preston". Under the leadership of a Northumberland squire, Thomas Foster, the Jacobites threw in the towel despite only some forty or so of their forces being killed or wounded, compared with three hundred of the Government forces. It surely must be one of the earliest examples of snatching defeat from the jaws of victory. Many of the Highlanders were rewarded for their treachery by being given free passage to the American colonies from where they could no longer pose a threat.

Two months after these disasters, on December 22nd, James Francis Edward Stuart arrived at Peterhead. The would-be monarch and the would-be kingmaker met at Fetteresso near Stonehaven. A court was convened at Scone, the traditional place for the coronation of Scottish kings. However, on hearing that government forces were approaching, the Jacobites abandoned Perth on 31st January 1716. On 4th February, Erksine – or Mar, call him what you will – along with the would-be James VIII or III, call *him* what you will, sailed from Montrose bound for France. Neither would see their home shores again. The earldom was attainted, unsurprisingly, but in exile, James created Erskine the Duke of Mar, to come into effect when he was more than just a king in name.

Mar did not rest on his laurels. In exile, he tried to raise funds for the cause. However, in 1721, it emerged he was getting an annual pension of £3,500 a year from George I. Bobbing again. The following year, he was also accused of betraying Bishop Francis Atterbury to the King, or to put it another way, earning his pension by revealing a plot whereby the Hanoverian family – lock, stock and barrel – would be taken prisoner and James pronounced king in his stead. Atterbury was sent to the Tower. As for Mar, after these two incidents, the Old Pretender, as he later came to be known, "had to let Mar go" as they say nowadays when someone has outlived their usefulness. Surprisingly, that only happened in 1724. What took him so long?

From Jacobite to Hanoverian, bobbing to the last, or nearly the last, Mar died at Aix-la-Chapelle in May 1732.

As for the castle, its story continues with John Farquharson (1673-1750), 9th Laird of Invercauld, who was captured at the Fight of Preston. Always a reluctant rebel, he had been sent to England to stir up rebellion. Not the best of choices, you would have thought. He was imprisoned in the Marshalsea, the infamous prison described by Dickens in *Little Dorrit*, and from where he wrote a grovelling letter to George I in which he used the word "humbling" no fewer than six times in the first sentence alone.

Anyway, it worked. He was released and is said to have kissed the hand of the King, in gratitude and as a gesture of loyalty. He was allowed to buy the ruined castle formerly belonging to his lords and masters and, in 1748, following the Battle of Culloden, it was rebuilt and leased to the government as a barracks for 99 years at £14 per annum as part of the measures to make sure there would be no more rebellions in the Highlands.

He may have become a loyalist, but his daughter, Lady Mackintosh, was not. She was married to Angus Mackintosh, Chief of the clan of that ilk, a Hanoverian and a captain in the Black Watch. She was only twenty-two years old when, hearing that Bonnie Prince Charlie had landed in Scotland, she raised, in his support, a regiment of about 400 men from her husband's clan and the

Chattan Confederation. They were in time to fight at the Battle of Falkirk on 17th January 1746.

A month later, on 16th February, to be precise, a grateful Prince was staying with her at Moy Hall just to the south of Inverness when word reached them that the commander of the Inverness barracks had sent out a party to arrest Charlie and claim the £30,000 that lay on his head. While the Prince skedaddled, Lady Anne's servants created a diversion in the garden, making such a racket that the dragoons thought their quarry was under the protection of a superior number of Jacobites and promptly retreated to the safety of the barracks without their prize. This episode has come down to history as the "Rout of Moy".

In a neat sequel, when Anne's husband, Angus, was captured by the Jacobites, the Prince handed him over to Anne, whom he called *La Belle Rebelle*, on the grounds that "he could not be in better security, or more honourably treated". Apparently when they were reunited, she famously greeted him with the words, "Your servant, captain" to which he replied, "Your servant, colonel". It's a very touching reunion and I would love it to be true, but it has a Hollywood sort of ring to it and I can't help but think that once the servants were out of earshot they had a right-good ding-dong. It's difficult to see how a marriage could survive such a fundamental difference of opinion. But it seemed it did.

Lady Mackintosh was arrested after the Jacobites' defeat at Culloden and put into the custody of her mother-in-law. A story goes that, accompanied by her husband, she later met the Duke of Cumberland at a ball in London. He asked her to dance to a government tune. Apart from butchering her clansmen and others at Culloden, as well as being immensely corpulent, the Lady must have felt she would rather die first but it was an offer she could hardly refuse. She agreed to dance with him as long as he danced to a Jacobite tune in return. *Touché.* She died on 2nd March 1784 at Leith.

That same year, the rebuilding of Braemar Castle got underway to the design of John, the son of William Adam, and his brother, Robert, who was to go on to become the foremost architect of his day. Adams were responsible for the design of the upper floors, heightening the cor-

Dungeon at Braemar Castle

ner turrets and giving them their present crenellations. They also strengthened the castle's defences by building a star-shaped curtain wall, as they did at Fort George (and where they were currently employed), the very latest thing in castle defence. It was also very well-connected. The new military road (now the A93) that ran from Fort George to Perth ran past the door.

The lower floors date from the 19th Earl's original L-shaped building with its spiral staircase, iron *yett* or gate, and pit prison. You can peer down into it through an iron grille where far below you can see a skeleton sitting in a zinc bath surrounded by coins. It looks like a scene from *Treasure Island* with pieces of eight glinting brightly.

In 1805, James Farquharson, the 10th Laird, died. Incredibly and very sadly, only one of his eleven children survived him. No-one deserves as much tragedy as that to fall into their lives. The survivor, against all the odds, was Catherine, who married James Ross of Balnagowan who, on the death of his father-in-law, adopted the Farquharson name.

In 1831, during the lifetime of his son, the 12th Laird, Braemar was returned to the Farquharsons who had been living at Invercauld Castle up till then. A new wing was added as servants' quarters, as well as a new kitchen. It was fit enough for a queen, and he did indeed entertain Queen Victoria when she attended the Braemar Gatherings which were held in the castle grounds at that time. The present Chief, and 16th Laird, is Captain Alwyne Compton Farquharson of Invercauld MC. He was born in 1919, and, as a very sprightly centenarian, in 2019, he attended his 71st consecutive Clan Gathering since becoming Chief.

And so, at long last in the castle's history, we come to the present day. In 2007, it was leased to the community for fifty years, the only community castle in all of Scotland. It is run by a local charity, Braemar Community Ltd., and is staffed by volunteers. Hats off to them. It's also why, if you can spare some loose change, you should toss it into the zinc bath in the pit prison, for you don't need to look too hard to see that the exterior of the castle needs some tender loving care and the sooner the better, knowing what ravages a Scottish winter can wreak. Actually, it is hoped, if enough funds can be raised, to

Drawing Room at Braemar Castle

begin restoration works in September 2020. They are expected to take eighteen months, which tells you just how much work needs to be done and how much money is needed. Then along came the coronavirus crisis and the castle had to temporarily close. No visitors means no cash coming in...

However, turning to the interior, there is no hint at all of the parlous state of the exterior

Dining Room at Braemar Castle

fabric of the building. Indeed, it looks quite the opposite – very homely, with lots of antique furniture including Hepplewhites, so I am reliably informed, though I couldn't care less about that. What does impress me, however, in the sort of way that some people like to be terrified out of their skins by watching a horror movie, is the bathroom. The enamel bath is equipped with antique taps and a Heath Robinson plug sort of contraption that might have been familiar to Noah.

The floor has a dizzying diamond pattern of black-and-white tiles, but it's the toilet that draws my eye with a sort of awful magnetism. I stare in disbelief that anyone would manufacture such a hideous object, far less that anyone would even dream of buying it. The porcelain is white but it has a gaudy pattern of blue flowers, not only on the outside, but the *inside* too. How strange the tastes of yesteryear! Never, in the history of water closets, has anything been so appropriately designed for the indignity of posterior uses.

If that was awful, by contrast, the dining room looks very civilised indeed with the table set as if the family might appear at any moment to devour whatever delicious repast cook and her team have prepared below stairs. Other rooms are fitted out with comfy-looking armchairs and squishy sofas with lots of photographs and portraits on the walls including one of Lady Anne. But that's not what interests me most – and feel free to disagree – but what I am attracted to are the large number of graffiti carved by the soldiers in the 18th century when the castle was used as a barracks. It's a terrible thing to deface property – and remember, this part of the castle was relatively new then, which makes it even worse. I certainly don't condone such vandalism, but on the other hand, standing here in the 21st century, standing where they stood when they carved their names, rank, regiment and the date into the wooden shutters, I feel I am in touch with their ghosts.

On that subject, no self-respecting castle would be complete without a ghost or two and Braemar has several. One story has it that on quiet nights, the sound of a baby's crying can sometimes be heard. It also dates back to the time of the barracks when a servant girl with a newborn baby was living there. Night after night, the little one refused to sleep and cried and cried and just would not settle. In a fit of anger and frustration at not being allowed to sleep himself, one of the soldiers snatched the babe from its bed and smashed its head against a wall.

In the 19th century, another tale tells of a honeymoon couple who had rented the castle to spend their wedding night. How romantic! In the morning, the bride awoke to find no husband by her side. She leapt to the conclusion that she had not pleased him the night before and he had deserted her. She also leapt from the highest turret and dashed her brains out on the ground below. A ghostly woman in a nightdress has sometimes been seen but the good news is, if ghosts spook you out, she is selective. She only reveals herself to newlyweds.

Most spooky of all, John Farquharson, aka the Black Colonel, has appeared in certain rooms. The shape of his body has been seen on the four poster bed, proof – if any were needed – that ghosts too get tired of haunting and need to lie down for a rest from time to time. And while you are there, see if you can detect the smell of tobacco on the air. If you do, that's due to him. He's either just left the room or, if it's pretty strong, he's there now watching you…

Chapter Eleven

Balmoral and Lochnagar: Much Ado about Royalty

AND so we come to Crathie Kirk, built from the local granite in the Gothic revival style and designed by A. Marshall Mackenzie, an architect from Elgin. It occupies the site of a former church where Victoria first came to worship in 1848 and continued to do so for the next 45 years. The new church was built by public funds including proceeds raised by a two-day bazaar held in the grounds of Balmoral by the Princesses Louise and Beatrice which, incredibly, raised £2,400 of the £6,000 needed.

The foundation stone was laid by the Queen in 1893, and the church was dedicated in 1895. She worshipped there for the last six years of her life, as the Royal Family still do to this day when they are staying at Balmoral. It's also where the Princess Royal was married in 1992. The south transept is reserved for the Royal Family while, in the north, you can warm your bottom on the pews of the Farquharsons and the Gordons. The latter are the owners of nearby Abergeldie Castle.

But not for us a visit to the kirk, though it seems to me, once upon a boyhood, I once did. Just as we were denied access to Mar Lodge, so we are denied access to the church. When you are down on your luck you really are down on your luck. Happily, I was not in need of a bit of a pray. Had we been able to gain access, we could have admired two stained glass windows presented by Queen Victoria and a communion table made of white marble

Crathie Kirk

from Iona, which was presented by George V. But not to worry, there is something else I *can* see which is open to the elements and which interests me much more.

From the hummock on which the church stands, I can see my goal, the churchyard and the ruins of the 15th century church of St Manire or Monire, an 8th century bishop of Aberdeenshire and Banff who, it is said, baptised his Pictish converts in a pool of the Dee near Balmoral and which to this day is known as "Polmanire". The pool and the churchyard lie only a short distance down a narrow road adjacent to the visitor centre car park.

Graveyard at Crathie Kirk

In the churchyard, bristling with tombstones, I find the one I have really come to see quite easily. My luck is beginning to change. On it is inscribed these words:

> *THIS STONE IS ERECTED*
> *IN AFFECTIONATE*
> *AND GRATEFUL REMEMBRANCE OF*
> *JOHN BROWN*
> *THE DEVOTED AND FAITHFUL*
> *PERSONAL ATTENDANT*
> *AND BELOVED FRIEND OF*
> *QUEEN VICTORIA*
> *IN WHOSE SERVICE HE HAD BEEN*
> *FOR 34 YEARS.*
> *BORN AT CRATHIENAIRD 8TH DECR. 1826*
> *DIED AT WINDSOR CASTLE 27TH MARCH 1883.*

The relationship between the *gillie* and the Queen is a story familiar to cinema-goers in the film *Mrs Brown*, so I will not go into that or speculate on just how close their relationship really was. There is nothing I could usefully add except to say that to visit the grave requires running the gauntlet of a good number of headstones with yellow plastic ribbons wrapped around them like bunting and bearing the legend in bold, black letters: *UNSAFE KEEP AWAY*.

John Brown's Gravestone

I suppose in these litigious times, you can't even rule out the dead coming back to get you.

John Brown is just one of the many servants or estate workers who are buried here. I won't mention them all but I must mention John Spong, the Queen's travelling *tapissier*, who was responsible for all the tapestries in the royal household. (One should never travel without one's *tapissier* – as Lady Bracknell didn't quite say – you just never know when you might need him.)

When Prince Albert bought Balmoral, the road on the south side of the river ran through the estate and met the road on the north side at Brig o' Dee, upriver, near Invercauld. It was hardly very private, the castle. Not something to which they were accustomed – having commoners passing through the policies without as much as by your leave. Accordingly, Albert commissioned the splendidly-named Isambard Kingdom Brunel (1806-59), the celebrated Victorian engineer, to build a bridge that would take vehicles across the river at the point where only a footbridge existed before. It was just a small project for he who had designed the SS *Great Western* (1837), the first purpose-built steamship for crossing the Atlantic, which she did in 1838; the SS *Great Britain* (1843), the largest passenger ship in the world until 1854; and the first iron ship to cross the Atlantic in 1845. He was to go on to design the SS *Great Eastern* (1859), the largest ship in the world at the time, capable of carrying 4,000 passengers from England to Australia without refuelling.

Actually, it was because of these achievements (not to mention many railway bridges), that he was given the commission. 130 foot long with criss-crossed latticework at the sides, the bridge was completed in 1857, the first single-span iron bridge in Scotland. Privacy was thus assured as traffic was diverted over the bridge onto the north side of the river. Brunel liked its "functional elegance", but the Queen was not amused. Presumably she wanted something much grander.

We drive over it to the lodge. It is here you can buy tickets to visit the castle, as long as you come between April and July. You can either walk from the car park or be taken from here in a trailer pulled by a Land Rover. Unfortunately for us, it is September; the Royal Family is in residence. However, the nice policeman with the automatic rifle allows me to park just long enough to pose in front of the ornamental wrought iron gates. He is part of the Royal Family's travelling protection unit and wheresoever they go, so does he. This makes me reflect for a moment on which would I rather be – a travelling *tapissier* with my needle and thread, or a bodyguard with my rifle and bullets? My new acquaintance tells me he's trained to an enormously high level, but he has never ever had to call his skills into action. Long may that continue.

Balmoral was bought in 1852 by Prince Albert as a present for the Queen. No greater love hath a man for his wife than he buy her a little place in the country. And it *was* just a little place, comparatively speaking, back then. It was a serendipitous event really. Victoria and Albert had been holidaying at Ardverikie on the shores of Loch Laggan in 1847 as the guests of James Hamilton, 2nd Marquess of Abercorn, who had the dubious honour of holding the title of "Groom of the Stool" to the Prince. I imagine it wasn't just the title he held for, as the name implies, his duties involved the disposal of the contents of the royal chamber pot. By this time, Victoria had been reigning supreme over the Empire for a decade and in that part of Scotland it was also raining, raining as if it would never cease, as she records in her diary. (A bit like RLS actually, who ended up in Braemar only because the weather was so dire in Pitlochry where he was holidaying – only in his case, it didn't get any better, so he was forced to stay indoors and put pen to paper, and thank God for that!)

Victoria's physician, Sir James Clark, informed the couple that at that very same time, his father was recuperating at Balmoral where the skies were blue. Albert decided that was where they needed to be and fortunately for him, a vacancy had recently arisen for the lease of the castle. Not so fortunate, however, for the previous tenant who had choked and died on a fish bone, thus creating the vacancy.

Balmoral Bridge

He was Robert Gordon, younger brother of the 4th Earl of Aberdeen, aka Lord Haddo, the future Prime Minister. He had acquired a long-term lease in 1830 from the 2nd Earl of Fife and made substantial alterations to the castle, demolishing most of it, if you please, and adding extensions in the baronial style. Albert took over the remaining 27 years left of the lease in 1848 without even hav-

Gates to Balmoral

ing seen the property, and in 1852 bought it and the 50,000-acre estate outright for £32,000. It sounds like the bargain of the century. That's about £3 million in today's money.

In the beginning, the estate at Balmoral was owned by Robert II (reigned 1371-90), who built a hunting lodge on it. In the year of the King's death, Sir William Drummond built a house. The following century, Alexander Gordon, the 3rd Earl of Huntly, built a fortified tower house which he sold in 1662 to the Farquharsons of Inverey. By 1746, they had added an extension. The 2nd Earl of Fife bought it in 1798. The rest you know.

When Victoria saw the castle for the first time, she thought it "small but pretty". She was right about the size. It was not fit for purpose. They had six children and still hadn't worked out what was causing them. She was to have three more.

Albert hired William Smith, the city architect of Aberdeen, to design a new castle and made some helpful "suggestions" himself. It was constructed in the very attractive silver-grey marble from a quarry on the Invergelder estate. The earlier castle was demolished, which seems a bit of a shame. A stone on the front lawn marks the place where the front door used to be.

Victoria laid the foundation stone for the new castle on 28th September 1853 (look for it on the adjacent wall to the west face of the entrance porch). Inside the cavity is a parchment signed by her, together with a representative from each of the current coins of the realm. In 1856, the castle was complete. Farm buildings and stables were added by 1859 and, at the time of his death of typhoid fever in 1861, Albert had been developing a model dairy along the lines of the one at Windsor.

Victoria's grief is well-documented, and she spent an increasing amount of her time in solitude at Balmoral. She continued the work on the dairy which was completed the following year. Other buildings followed over the years, so there are now 150 of them including *Baile-na-Coille* (the farm of the wood), the cottage built for John Brown. Some cottage! It looks very grand with its roof projecting over the windows, Tyrolean style. It was probably designed by William Smith, aforesaid, with additions by Sir Robert Rowand Anderson in 1904/05 and with further alterations in 1923/24. Alas, it was incomplete at the time of Brown's death in 1883 so, unfortunately for him, he never occupied it. He probably lived in the "Croft", built in 1858; a mini version of *Baile-na-Coille*.

In a similar vein, another building of interest is the cottage the Queen built for her Indian Secretary, Abdul Karim (1863-1909), aka "the Munshi", which means "clerk" or "teacher". Very graciously, the Queen allowed him to bring his wife over from India, and Victoria named the cottage "Karim" in his honour. He spared no expense in decorating it to his own taste, and threw a housewarming for the royal household when it was ready.

The relationship between "the Munshi" and the Queen was entirely platonic, of that we can be sure, despite them spending the night together in a remote part of the estate at what she called her "widow's house", *Glas-allt-Shiel* ("green [or grey] lodge on the stream") on Loch Muick in 1889, two years after his arrival. He was 26, she was 70, and so even with the worst will in the world, it's hard to imagine anything of the improper sort going on. All the same, it's no wonder that the tongues began to wag because not since John Brown's days had anyone been so favoured. In fact, it was the first time she had spent the night in the house since Brown's death.

The Munshi's rapid rise to favour did not go down well with the rest of the royal household. After his mother's death, her son, now King Edward VII, instructed that all their correspondence and photographs be destroyed. It wasn't racism – or at least, not entirely. He had issued the same orders after the death of John Brown.

When the Queen died in 1901, Karim was given a place of honour in the funeral procession. It was all for show. After it was over, he was ordered to hand over every letter Victoria had ever written to him so they could be consumed by fire. I find it rather amusing to reflect that when Edward was a young man, his mother heartily disapproved of *his* behaviour, while he in turn heartily disapproved of *hers* in her later years!

Fortunately, some photographs of the Queen and "the Munshi" together have survived, and well as some letters from her to him in which she signs herself off as "your affectionate mother, VRI" and "your truly devoted and fond loving mother, VRI". And there you have it – it was more a mother-and-son relationship than anything imagined by prurient minds.

Apart from a road no longer running through it, privacy at the castle was enhanced when, under the guidance of the landscape gardener, James Beattie, trees were planted, including exotic conifers. Parterres were also laid out, all of which Albert took a keen interest in. When he saw a prefabricated iron cottage at the Great Exhibition in 1851, he ordered that a temporary ballroom and dining room be constructed of the same material at Balmoral. It first saw service that year and served until 1856 when the "real" ballroom was ready. Thus began the Gillies' Ball, a tradition that continues to this day, twice a year.

The ballroom is also used for temporary exhibitions and features permanent displays of fine china, paintings by Landseer (1802-73), and silver sculptures by Sir Joseph Boehm (1834-90) who, as well producing several statues of Victoria, most famously designed the 1887 Jubilee head on the coinage. His initials "JEB" are inconspicuous just beneath the shoulder. Sadly, the design was widely criticised and the coin was replaced in 1893.

After Victoria died in 1901, Balmoral was inherited by Edward VII who only came for three or four weeks a year. His son, George V, inherited both the throne and Balmoral in 1910, but it would have been undiplomatic to come here to idyllic Deeside for his holidays while the First World War was raging in the mud of Flanders Fields, so they didn't. But for all that, he did leave his mark on it. He it was who commissioned, from local craftsmen, the wrought iron gates at the entrance, while the three-acre flower garden was designed by his consort, Queen Mary, between 1923-25. It was also a time of modernisation for the castle. Electricity was installed, powered by a turbine and generators courtesy of the Gelder Burn.

In 1937, it was the turn of George VI to inherit the castle until his untimely death in 1952, when our present Queen took over. Queen Mary's garden was extended by the Duke of Edinburgh to create a kitchen garden to provide vegetables for the family's table. He also created a walk bordered by flowers along the north terrace and a water garden to the south-west. Finally, he began a plantation of oaks. You can never have too many trees these days to mitigate the effects of global warming and a rich carbon dioxide atmosphere.

It was here that Prince Charles spent his honeymoon with Diana and it was where, in 1997, their two sons heard of their mother's tragic death. There have been happy times and there have been sad times at Balmoral.

And so, saying thanks and farewell to my friendly policeman, we continue along the south side of the river on the B796 until we come to the sign where the road leads uphill to the Royal Lochnagar distillery. It offers five different tours with prices to match the experience. We find it

Royal Lochnagar Distillery

open, but reader, alas, we do not have time to pay a visit. As Robert Frost almost said: "We have miles to go to before we sleep."

The first legal distillery was founded in 1823 on the north bank of the Dee by James Robertson, who had been operating illicitly long before that. It mysteriously burned down in 1826. The finger of suspicion points at his former fellow illicit distillers who were a bit miffed, to put it mildly, at his decision to turn legit.

The indefatigable Robertson built another distillery in the foothills of Lochnagar. Lightning struck again in 1841 when that too burned down – not that I'm suggesting it was the culprit, by any means. A third distillery was built in 1845 on the south bank by John Begg. It was a smart move when he invited the new neighbours at Balmoral to pay a visit, warning them that they would need to arrive before 6pm if they wanted to see the process in operation. As anyone who has ever visited a distillery knows, watching whisky being made and matured is a bit like watching paint dry. Obviously, Begg was not making any special concessions for his prestigious guests.

He must have been delighted when the very next day, the Queen, Albert, and their three eldest children turned up unannounced. Begg had unwittingly tapped into a rich vein. The young couple were rather fond of the country's national drink. If he was surprised, I am astonished. I had never imagined Victoria as a whisky drinker, somehow. Intrigued, I delved further into the subject and discovered she committed the sin of mixing it with claret. Dearie, wearie me!

Location is everything, and being so near Balmoral, the distillery has been visited over the years by the great and the good, from far and wide, including Prime Ministers of every stripe, on their day off after meeting the monarch at Balmoral. In 1963 a major reconstruction took place, and in 1990 a visitor centre was built.

Now part of the Diageo empire (actually the smallest distillery in its portfolio), some of its production of 450,000 litres a year goes into the Johnnie Walker Black Label and the prestigious Blue Label. In 2004, however, 6,000 bottles of a 30-year-old cask strength were released as part of the Rare Malts series. A 70cl bottle will set you back a mere £3,999.90. I'm glad about the 90p. You have no idea how much difference 10p makes when you are spending almost £4,000 on a bottle of malt.

As for the name "Lochnagar", as many of you probably know, Prince Charles was inspired to write a story, *The Old Man of Lochnagar* (1980), when he was staying at Balmoral in order to entertain his two younger brothers. Long before that, in 1807, Byron wrote *Lachin y Gair* or *Dark Lochnagar* in which he celebrates his roots in the north-east. His ancestor, William Gordon, was the third son of George, 2nd Earl of Huntly, and Anabella Stuart, daughter of James I of Scotland, no less.

It sounds more like a loch than the mountain of 3,789 feet it actually is. That's due to a mix-up with a *lochan* in one of the corries called *Lochan na Gaire* meaning "little loch of the noisy sound". So now you know.

What you may not know is that a lesser-known and alternative name for the mountain is *Beinn Chiochan* (Mountain of the Beasts). I am fine with that, but less sanguine with the fact that the summit is sometimes referred to as *Cac Càrn Beag*. By any other name it would smell as bad. It means "little cairn of cack" – little heap of poo. (Other, less polite, names for "poo" are available.)

Chapter Twelve

Abergeldie and Birkhall: A Tale of Two Castles

TWO miles from Balmoral, along the A93 to Ballater, stands Abergeldie Castle on the south bank of the Dee. It is a four-storey tower house, presently the home of Baron Abergeldie. It has been in the hands of the Gordon family for 600 years, but that nearly came to an end in the floods of January 2016 when the river ate away 250 feet of the river bank and the water came lapping at the back door. The Baron and his wife were forced to flee. For a while the castle teetered on the brink of collapsing into the river, but fortunately engineers were able to save the day, and the castle, by building a massive barricade of boulders to shore up the bank.

The Gordons first acquired the lands in 1482 and the castle was probably built about 1550 by Sir Alexander Gordon, the 4th Laird and son of the 1st Earl of Huntly. In 1562, he was bound over to keep the peace on a penalty of 5,000 merks. He went on to fight for the Earl of Huntly in 1594, regardless. He was succeeded by his son, William, who was one of a number of Catholics involved in a plot against James VI. Not the Gunpowder one.

During the Jacobite rising of 1689, the castle was besieged by the Jacobites, but after their defeat at the Battle of Cromdale on 1st May 1690, the siege was lifted by General Hugh Mackay of Scourie at the head of 1,400 Dutch infantry. The castle was in the wars again in the Rebellion of 1715 when it was garrisoned by Government troops, and again in the short-lived Rising of 1719, when it was occupied by Spanish troops.

A wing was added in the 18th century, but demolished in 1969. And talking of demolition, if you want to get an idea of what the castle that Albert pulled down to replace with Balmoral looked like, then take a close look at Abergeldie. They were identical twins. On the lawn in front of the house is a standing stone over six feet high and nearly three feet wide. It's another re-

Abergeldie Castle

minder, as if any were needed, that the Gordons are newcomers to this ancient landscape.

At the same time that he bought Balmoral, Albert also bought a forty-year lease on the Abergeldie estate. In the event, the lease only came to an end in 1970. Not only that, but Albert also bought the nearby Birkhall estate of 6,500 acres, though according to a contemporaneous rumour, the laird lost it in a card game. Whatever the truth of that may be, it is certainly the case that Albert had very deep pockets.

After his marriage in 1863 to Princess Alexandra of Denmark, Edward VII came to Abergeldie every year for his summer holidays which he spent blasting birds out of the sky and killing deer. When he wasn't doing that, he spent the time fishing and playing cards and, on one occasion, entertaining Gladstone who was staying at Balmoral.

The Queen's mother, the Duchess of Kent, was a frequent visitor from 1850-56 and in 1879, the Princess Eugénie (1826-1920), wife of Napoleon III and the last Empress of France, came here in the October of 1879 to mourn the death of her son, the Prince Imperial, who was killed in a skirmish in the Anglo-Zulu war. He was only twenty-three. Then, when Edward ascended the throne in 1901, it was used by his family, the future George V and his daughters, the Princesses Louise, Victoria and Maud of Wales.

I am pleased to report it has a ghost – a woman called Catherine or Kitty Rankie, aka "French Kate", a servant accused of being a witch. She was held prisoner in the cellars and burned at the stake at *Creag-na-Ban* or "Rock of the Women" which overlooks the castle. Her ghost is said to haunt the cellars and the clock tower.

As for Birkhall, from the Scots *Birk Hauch,* meaning "birch river-meadow", it was built in 1715 and originally owned by the Farquharsons who sold it to the Gordons, who sold it to Prince Albert (or lost it in a card game).

He, generous as ever, gave it to his son and heir, the Prince of Wales, aka "Bertie". However, his mother removed it from him in 1885 (not that it was hers to take away, I would have said), some say because of his dissolute lifestyle of which she heartily disapproved. Because of his many affairs, some wag christened him "Edward the Caresser". Actually it's much more likely that he was dispossessed, firstly because he only used it once, preferring Abergeldie Castle, and secondly because the Queen needed it to house her burgeoning family – and staff to take care of them, of course.

In the 1930s, George V kindly loaned the property to the Duke and Duchess of York who stayed there in the summer, along with their two daughters. They redecorated it and replanted the gardens. When the Duke unexpectedly became George VI in 1936, they used Balmoral but their older grown-up daughter, Elizabeth, and her husband, Philip, continued to holiday at Birkhall.

Birkhall

When the Queen Mother died in 2002, Charles, Prince of Wales, inherited it. (One should always choose one's grandmother carefully and make sure you are the first born, to boot. It's not easy, but it should be attempted whenever conceivably possible.) He spent his second honeymoon here in 2005, and Prince William and Catherine celebrated New Year's Eve there in 2011. They knew, as the world does, that no-one celebrates New Year like the Scots.

If you can stop on your way to Ballater to admire Abergeldie from the other side of the river, then take a moment to lift your eyes south-west to the hills where you will see something extraordinary. (Actually, you can't miss it if you are driving west, silhouetted as it is against the skyline.)

It looks as if it has been transplanted from Egypt. It's actually a pyramid-shaped cairn on top of Craig Lurachain. And on that cairn there is a plaque which reads: TO THE BELOVED MEMORY OF ALBERT THE GREAT AND GOOD PRINCE CONSORT. ERECTED BY HIS BROKEN HEARTED WIDOW VICTORIA R. 21st AUGUST 1862.

Another inscription runs round the pyramid: HE BEING MADE PERFECT IN A SHORT TIME, FULFILLED A LONG TIME. FOR HIS SOUL PLEASED THE LORD THEREFORE HASTENED HE TO TAKE HIM AWAY, FROM THE WICKED. WISDOM OF SOLOMON IV.13.14.

Well, that's a ringing endorsement if ever I heard one. In fact, I get the feeling that Albert must be blushing in heaven.

The tradition of erecting cairns on the Balmoral estate began with the Purchase Cairn in 1852 on the summit of Craig Gowan. As Victoria tells us in her journals, she placed the first stone, Albert the second, then the children, then the household until it was some seven feet high. Albert placed the last stone at the top and all the while a piper played, whisky was drunk, and there was much mirth and dancing.

Another cairn commemorates the expansion of the estate in 1878, and there are others to commemorate the marriages of the "children" on Canup hill. Edward's cairn is on the Birkhall estate. However, there is none to commemorate, in 1874, the marriage of Alfred to the Grand Duchess Maria Alexandrova of Russia, daughter of Alexander II. Instead, Peak Freans, the London bakers, created a biscuit in her honour which they named "Marie".

So no cairn for Alfred, only something named after his wife that goes soggy when you dunk it in your tea. I don't know what Alfred made of that as a memorial, but I wouldn't be surprised if he thought it rather took the biscuit.

Chapter Thirteen

Ballater: The Station and the Shops

IN 1866, the railway line, operated by the Aboyne and Braemar Railway Company, which had previously terminated at Aboyne, was extended to Ballater. It not only facilitated Victoria's visits to Balmoral, but also provided a boost for the town as her subjects came in their droves to see what was drawing their Queen to the area. It was also very convenient for her guests such as the Shah of Persia who came in 1889, and Tsar Nicholas II in 1896.

The station lasted for a hundred years, longer than many rural stations, before Baron Beeching wielded his axe. It did, however, see a new lease of life as an exhibition centre featuring the royal connection with the area. Unfortunately, a fire broke out in the early hours of 12th May 2015 and the building was destroyed. Fortunately, a replica of the royal carriage was spared – but only just.

The good news is that out of the ashes arose another visitor centre, better than before, with information for tourists about the connections with royalty, visitor attractions, a library and the Royal Waiting Room. In addition, there is a café, a classy tearoom and a bistro which collectively go under the name of "The Carriage". Another feature which I think has been to the good, is that the bold fire-engine red of the wooden facings of the buildings at the time of the conflagration have been repainted with the original pale green. What a difference a change of paint-colour makes! It is rather reminiscent of the Duke of Rothesay Pavilion in Braemar, light and extremely elegant, seeming to almost float, whereas that red (which I've seen in photographs), really seems to weigh it down.

Ballater Visitor Centre

In the beginning, the station was just a single platform with a booking office, but after some consultation with Her Majesty, a waiting room was built in 1886. On its centenary, our present Queen visited it and, according to tradition, inspected the Royal Guard in front of the station. I am sure the soldiers all passed muster. Look carefully at the surface of the road on the other side of the car park and you will see, embedded in it, some initials all beginning with "GN" followed by two more letters. They mean nothing to me but, in Victoria's day, it told those about to be inspected where precisely they had to stand.

Railway Carriage at Ballater Visitor Centre

As photographs inside the centre show, Victoria was transported by carriage to Balmoral, and I am damn sure she would rather have just got on with getting there rather than having to inspect the troops. And if she thought *that*, you can bet your bottom dollar that the poor foot soldiers who would have been assembled in their serried ranks long before her arrival, hanging about in the rain (most probably) waiting for the Royal Train to arrive (almost certainly late), would endorse that sentiment entirely. We each have our jobs to do. Some jobs are better than others. Some come with perks. Some don't.

Apart from receiving the Royal Family more or less annually until 1965 (the last royal journey from Ballater took place at 7.15pm on 15th October), the station unwittingly became involved in a scandal when Mrs Wallis Simpson stepped onto the platform in September 1936 before being whisked off to Balmoral to join her friend, Edward VIII. The trouble was that he had been scheduled to open the new infirmary at Foresterhill in Aberdeen. He pleaded he was still in mourning after the death of his father on 20th January and delegated his younger brother, the future George VI, to do the job instead. I'm sure when Mrs Simpson arrived safely at Balmoral, she was a great comfort to the new King.

Arguably, the star of the visitor centre is the Royal Train's saloon car with its gleaming black-and-white livery and coats of arms on the side. A peek though the windows reveals plush sofas and chairs and velvet drapery, fit for a Queen, just as you would expect, but most impressive of all are the rosette lights, flush in the padded ceiling. On the roof, the paraffin lanterns stand up proud like pimples and I imagine when the train was in motion, it scattered showers of sparks behind it.

Royal Waiting Room

Tables and chairs from the bistro spill out onto the platform in front of the carriage but, further along, you can also choose to sit and eat at – and I really like this – booths with high-backed, red-leather seats, a couple of oblong mirrors framed in wooden panels above them, and this is the *coup de grâce* – a net luggage rack. Apart from the (necessary) table between the seats, it is easy to imagine you really are sitting in a railway carriage.

Even better, in each compartment are a couple of framed copies of those wonderfully evocative railway posters churned out by the railway companies in the golden age of railway travel from the Thirties to the Fifties. They feature locomotives shovelling steam over their shoulders, mountain scenery and, not least, the attractions of the resorts to which they are whisking you in comfort. They truly are works of art. I love them, though bizarrely, some of the artists were rather ashamed of prostituting their art for such shameless commercialism and signed their work off with pseudonyms. Between them, a lamp on the wall shines its light on the coat of arms of the Great North of Scotland Railway Company.

And if that is quite splendid, you ain't seen nothing yet, as Al Jolson didn't quite say. The Queen's waiting room really takes the breath away. It's incredibly opulent with its wooden panelling and stained-glass windows, every inch the Victorian dining room, complete with an aspidistra on a stand in the corner. Running down the centre of the table are candelabra bristling with candles, while it is set with gleaming silver cutlery and crystal glasses (three per place-setting) that sparkle like diamonds.

By contrast, the grate looks gloomy but when a fire was burning merrily in it, it would have been very cheery. I can't say I approve of the upholstery on the chairs, however. The pattern is far too loud and gaudy for my taste – but then, when the diners were seated, they would have covered it up.

It's for show only, but if you

Tearoom, Ballater

are in need of a bite to eat, next door is the much-less-fussy tearoom with a delicate floral pattern on the upholstery and bone china plates and cups and saucers. Very elegant. This is where you might take someone for a treat on their birthday or to mark a special occasion.

Across from the station car park are the Albert Memorial Hall and the Victoria Hall. They were the gifts of Alexander Gordon (1818-95).

The Albert Memorial Hall, Ballater

He was a local lad who, like Dick Whittington, went to London to make his fortune, and did. He owned two breweries in the capital. The Albert Hall opened in 1874 and the Victoria Hall and Gordon Institute followed in 1895, the year of his death, as you may have noticed. And that was not all by any means. This remarkable benefactor also built a bridge at Polhollick, two miles to the west, in 1892, and ten years after his death, the suspension bridge at Cambus o' May, three miles to the east, was built using funds provided by him. He is also supposed to have contributed to the building of Glenmuick Church in the centre of the town.

The inscription at the corner of the Albert Hall is somewhat fulsome. Below Albert's name and dates, it reads:

A PRINCE INDEED
ABOVE ALL TITLES A HOUSEHOLD WORD
HEREAFTER THROUGH ALL TIME
ALBERT THE GOOD

No prizes for guessing who gave the Royal Consent to that, if she did not pen it herself!

In 1850, a temporary barracks was built to house the Queen's Guard, composed from a detachment of the 53rd Sutherland Highlanders, to protect her when she was staying at Balmoral. In 1869, a row of Elizabethan cottages were converted into a permanent barracks and in 1904, some flat-roofed oriental buildings were added. It was alleged that they were intended for India but ended up here apparently as the result of a blunder. Given that flat roofs and the Scottish climate are not the best of bedfellows, the story may well have some substance.

The barracks is situated on Queens Road, appropriately enough. The buildings are hemmed in by white iron railings and, peering through them, I can see the compound extends as far as the eye can see. It looks as big as a village, but there is not a single soul to be seen. Only, and it comes as a bit of a surprise to see, on the wall this side of the railings, a cock pheasant is looking quite at home in this ur-

Ballater Barracks

ban environment. It is September and we know the moors are not the safest place for pheasants at this time of year. It would seem this smart bird has sussed that out and reckons there is safety in the streets of Ballater where the citizens do not go about toting shotguns.

Perhaps he has flown in from the 1,319 foot Craigendarroch ("Hill of Oaks"), at Ballater's back door. You can climb it if you like, while those seeking a more serious sort of exercise can take a seven-mile hike to Loch Muick and from there head for the heady heights of the 3,789 foot-high Lochnagar. Having reached the top, like the Duke of York's men, you can march back down again (well maybe not march), then walk the seven miles back to your accommodation in Ballater. A nice wee stroll.

For those who prefer to bike rather than hike, Ballater is the western terminus of the 41-mile Deeside Way which ends at Duthie Park in the centre of Aberdeen. (Other trails in the area are available, such as those in the forests of Cambus o' May.)

As you go around the town, you cannot fail to notice the large number of "By Appointment" signs on the exterior of a number of shops. They are "Royal Warrants", currently granted on behalf of the Queen, the Duke of Edinburgh and the Prince of Wales. Those granted by the Queen Mother elapsed five years after her death in 2007, as the rules dictate. They are only awarded to tradesmen and companies, never to professionals or places of entertainment such as theatres and pubs. It takes a minimum of five years of supplying goods and services to the Royal Family before the supplier's claim can even be considered by the Royal Household Warrants Committee. If the request is accepted, then it goes to the grantor, that is to say the royal personage, for final ratification.

You can imagine it does no harm at all to your business to have the coat of arms of the grantor and "By appointment" followed by the name of the goods or services you provided displayed on the wall of your establishment. Which reminds me – according to *Scotland the What?* there is a toy shop, by appointment to Lady Diana, supplier of *futrets* to her sons when they were small. The furry little creatures (known as ferrets to those who don't speak the Doric), were supposedly knitted by a *wifie* in Hong Kong.

Haven't come across it yet. Now, I wonder where it could be…

Chapter Fourteen

Beyond Ballater: Wonderful Water, Knights Templar and Knights of the Road

IN the times of the Templars, there were ancient trackways along the Dee which determined the locations of settlements and castles at strategic points along the valley. Ballater was one such settlement, commanding the Dee Valley and Glen Gairn which runs north to Strathdon. That indefatigable builder of bridges, Thomas Telford, built a bridge here in 1809. It had a short life span, being washed away in floods twenty years later. It was back to the ferry for folks until a replacement bridge was built five years later.

Ballater unexpectedly got a boost round about 1760 when it became a spa town, accommodating visitors going to the Pannanich mineral well on the south side of the Dee. The Templars knew of its existence, but the history of the well really began when a local woman, Elspet (or Isabella) Michie was somehow inspired to drink from the springs and bathe in their waters. Her neighbours thought she had lost the plot as the water was rather chilly. She was suffering from scrofula or tuberculosis of the lymph node, popularly known in those days as the "king's evil". She had the last laugh, however, when as a result of taking the treatment, she was completely cured.

The Old Pannanich Inn

And so the fame of the curative powers of the waters grew as tales of other miraculous cures followed. Enter the entrepreneurial Francis Farquharson, the 6th Laird of Monaltrie, who built an inn, bathhouses and a granite memorial from which the water still flows. The people came to be cured of rheumatism, consumption, typhus, scarlet fever and scores of other fevers.

Farquharson was a cousin of Colonel Anne, aka *La Belle Rebelle*, and like her, a supporter of Bonnie Prince Charlie. He raised three hundred men for his cause and fought at the Battles of Inverurie, Falkirk and Culloden. He was said to be very handsome with golden locks. Beauty is of course in the eye of the beholder and I couldn't comment on how good-looking he might have been, but I have to say "Bonnie" does seem to fit the Prince perfectly as in his portraits he looks extremely effeminate, though of course in actuality he was as heterosexual as a pedigree bull.

Francis was captured at Culloden, sent to the Tower of London and sentenced to death, only to be reprieved on 28th November 1746, the very day set for his execution. The rumour went around that it was due to the intercession of a certain lady at court who had some influence. She may, or may not, have been Margaret Eyre of Hessop in Derbyshire. Whatever the truth of that may be – reader, he married her many years later, in 1763.

Spared but not pardoned, he spent some time afterwards in the clink, including the Marshalsea, before ultimately being released on parole which restricted him to a ten-mile radius of Berkhamstead. It was to be twenty years before he was finally pardoned and able to return to Deeside with his bride. Fortunately she was a lady in possession of a large fortune and he was able to build himself a new mansion which he called "Ballater House", his previous home having been burnt to the ground in reprisal for his support of the Lad who would be King. In 1784, he was able to buy back his estates for £16 13/- 9d. He died in 1790, aged 80, and was buried in the old Kirkyard at Crathie.

What Farquharson built, Jonathan Troup, a surgeon from Aberdeen, cashed in on. In the 1790s, he placed adverts in the *Aberdeen Journal* and was on hand to advise on how often, when, and how big a dose should be, and how to bathe in the waters.

In 1795, a local minister, the Reverend Dr John Ogilvie, who fancied himself as bit of a rhymer, penned these lines:

> *I've seen the auld seem young and frisky,*
> *Without the aid of ale or whisky,*
> *I've seen the dullest hearts grow brisky*
> *At blithesome, helpful Pannanich.*

The great and the good came here too, including Lord Byron who came round about that time as a child. He had a deformed right foot, and perhaps his mum took him there hoping for a cure. They had a contentious relationship to say the least. He disapproved of her drinking and mocked her for being short and fat, to which she retaliated on one occasion by calling him a "lame brat".

Other famous visitors were Sir Walter Scott who came in 1822 and John Brown, *the* John Brown, who worked in the hotel stables before he moved on to greater things. Last, and certainly not least, was his boss, Queen Victoria, who took along some of her guests who were staying at Balmoral.

And here's something to reflect on as you drink it – it's fifty years old. That's how long it takes to see the light of day again after the gentle rain (and sometimes not so gentle) falls upon the hills and is filtered through cracks in the rock. It's this filtering process that gives the water its unique properties.

Well, to tell you the truth, it's not really a well at all, but rather three natural artesian springs where the water comes to the surface under its own pressure. Analysis shows the waters drawn from the different springs are all very similar.

The inn which the entrepreneurial Mr Farquharson founded has been converted into private residences now. However, when it was an inn, in one of the bedrooms, some visitors reported having heard breathing – though there was nothing to be seen. Let me tell you that would freak me out much more than the sight of a ghostly apparition. Others have reported a scent of violets, which I think would be rather nice and not in the least scary. A grey lady, dressed like a maid, has also been sighted. I can't help but wonder where the ghosts are now. Are they homeless, or roaming their former home, somewhat confused, not a little put out at these domestic changes?

The amount of consumption of the water has changed out of all recognition from those early days. The Deeside Water Company, founded in 1996, stands on the B976 opposite the former inn. It is from here that the water, both still and sparkling, is bottled at an incredible 5,000 bottles an hour before being distributed to a supermarket near you, as well as outlets in Europe and Asia. In 1998, the water was officially recognised both in the UK and EU as a natural mineral water. And you needn't worry about supplies running dry any time soon. It flows all year round, and more than a billion litres of rain fall upon the one square mile around the springs every year.

I'm not going to get too scientific with you, but the Deeside water has anti-oxidant properties – and that's important, because they help reduce the effects of free radicals which speed up cell damage and the ageing process. But don't just take my word for it. No fewer that eleven research studies in universities, hospitals and laboratories have proven this to be a fact.

The water also has anti-inflammatory properties, which help rheumatism and recovery from sports injuries. And get this: it's not just good for your innards – it's good for your skin too. In tests conducted at Leeds Skin Centre in

2009, volunteers who drank a litre of Deeside Water a day increased their skin hydration by 23% and reduced the appearance of wrinkles by 17%. Isn't that an amazing thing! One thing it does not seem to be able to do, however, is cure a broken heart. Queen Victoria drank gallons of it and it never cured hers. Strange to reflect that what she drank at the end of her long reign fell as rain the first time she first visited the well.

We continue along the B976 until we reach the B9158, which takes us over the river to Dinnet where we pick up the A93 again and head back towards Ballater. Just before Cambus o' May (from *Camas a' Mhuigh,* "the river bend on the plain"), three miles east of Ballater, is the suspension bridge funded by Alexander Gordon. It was badly damaged after Storm Frank blew up on 30th December 2015. Graeme Miller couldn't believe his eyes when he saw a residential caravan stuck under it. He caught on camera the moment when another caravan struck it and both floated downstream. They were the advance guard: the entire park was swept downstream.

Meanwhile, in Ballater, the flooding reached biblical proportions. The Dee burst its banks at the golf course and spilled onto the streets and into people's houses and businesses. It affected 600 of the former and 100 of the latter. And it wasn't just Ballater and the North-East that was affected; all of Britain was. Not since Noah's time had such high waters been experienced. Meanwhile, the North Pole was experiencing something of a heatwave, +1°C compared to the normal -28°C. And some mumpsimuses say there is no such thing as global warming!

The cost of repairs to the bridge is estimated to be in the region of £400,000. Prince Charles has pledged an undisclosed sum towards it, while Aberdeen Council has committed £250,000. The rest will be raised by community fundraising.

At Cambus o' May, we stop at AA Patrol box No. 472, only one of sixteen such boxes still *in situ* throughout the entire country and which has been lovingly maintained by a bunch of dedicated volunteers. I'm sure younger folk will be underwhelmed, but it's a wonderful piece of nostalgia for me. It takes me back to my boyhood, when my father was a member of the AA, and when the membership badge which you fixed to the front grille of your

AA Patrol Box at Cambus o' May

car was a real metal badge with cursive letters, not the anodyne sort of logo the AA trades under these days. Members were issued with a key which allowed them access to boxes like this. A great idea, and even better if you happened to break down in the vicinity of one.

Inside the box is a display of old black-and-white photos, mainly of men and machines, including an impressive one of a convoy, looking rather military it has to be said, and a very curious one of a man with a moustache standing beside a bicycle with an AA badge pinned to his chest bearing the number 180. He is attired in a *bunnet*, starched stiff collar and black tie, a jacket with many pockets, jodhpurs, and a black armband on the left sleeve. With no tools, it's difficult to see what practical purpose he could serve, apart from conducting a service of the dead over the conked-out engine when he finally managed to arrive at the scene. No doubt that was the reason for the black armband. Like the Boy Scouts, he was prepared.

There are also some colour photos showing the state the box was in before restoration (very bad) and a couple of others with vintage cars posing in front of it. Another snap taken after the restoration had been completed shows the restorers with an engineer on his bike, just as he would have been in the days of yore. Great job, gentlemen!

These modern-day medieval knights of the road were attired in a light-brown uniform and sat astride their steeds whose sidecar, I imagine, contained a bag of tricks which could solve mechanical faults of the most common and less serious sort. Always on the move, they covered endless miles, perpetually on the lookout – not for damsels in distress, but for motorists experiencing a mechanical breakdown.

And another thing: they had to be constantly on the alert to salute members whom they happened to encounter on the road. We could see them coming in their distinctive uniform and rig long before it was possible for *them* to spot our little badge on the front of our car. We would keenly watch the AA man's approach to see if he saluted us. He always did, and it seems to me it happened with such regularity that the roads must have been very well-patrolled. A map in the box shows how they covered every corner of the country. A glory hath passed away from the earth.

Before coming back to Ballater, we stop to visit the cemetery and ruins of Tullich Kirk. It was abandoned in 1798 when a new parish church was built to serve the three parishes of Glenmuick, Tullich and Glencairn. But much earlier than that, St Nathalan – or Nachalan, or Neachtan (d. 678) – founded the first church here in the mid 600s.

Born in Tullich, he was a rich landowner who generously gave his crops to the poor. One story tells how he once gave away all his seed corn to the

Ruins of Tullich Kirk

peasants and sowed sand instead. Believe it or not, from it, all kinds of grain sprouted forth. And if you find *that* hard to believe, then try this tale for size.

One rainy day he cursed the rain that was ruining his crops. He was probably thinking of the plight of the starving poor, but later he realised he had done a terrible thing because the rain was God's creation and who was he, a mere mortal, to criticise his Maker? What could he do to atone for this terrible sin? Nathalan had an idea. He padlocked his right arm to his right leg, tossed the key into the Dee and set out to walk all the way to Rome and seek a pardon from the Pope. Once he got there, the first thing he did was to buy a fish at the market. When he cut it open, you'll never guess what he found inside. Yes, that's right, the key to the padlock! It was surely a sign from God that he was forgiven. The Pope was impressed and decided to make him a bishop. A pool near the church he founded is called the "key pool" in homage of this event. Nathalan's bones are supposed to lie somewhere in the kirkyard.

Before that fateful day, however, he went on to found two more churches. Today, the Roman Catholic church in Ballater is named after him, as is the Masonic Lodge – number 259 on the roll of Grand Lodges of Scotland.

Jump forward six centuries or so to the next stage of the kirk's story, to the days of David I when it was in the care of the Knights Templar, or to give them their full handle: The Poor Fellow-Soldiers of Christ and of the Temple of Solomon. So far, so good. Then along came Friday 13th October 1307. It was a very bad day for the Knights Templar. In fact, it has been suggested that the events of that day gave rise to the superstition that Friday 13th is a day when you can expect bad luck to befall you.

At daybreak on that day, all over France, Templars were dragged out of bed and arrested. Their big mistake was to fall foul of Philip IV of France (reigned 1285-1314), aka *Philippe le Bel* (Philip the Fair), or the Iron King. "Fair" is a word normally applied to the gentler sex, but the second soubriquet was well-deserved. In 1306, Philip expelled the Jews, seized their property and confiscated the monies owed to them. A year later, on that black day aforesaid, he arrested more than six hundred Templars on fake charges of heresy, sodomy, usury, fraud and immorality, to name but five.

Philip's hostility to both groups was because he was massively in debt to them. The Templars' original role was to protect pilgrims on their crusades to the East but, by the end of the 13th century, they had got into banking and other business enterprises. Under torture, they admitted the heresy and many of them were burned at the stake. Under threat of military action from Philip, at the Council of Vienne in 1311, Pope Clement V – the first Avignon pope – was forced to abolish the Order.

Philip's instruction to his fellow monarchs in Europe to deal with the Templars in like manner was not pursued as enthusiastically as he did. They more-or-less painlessly morphed into the Knights Hospitallier of the Order of St John. In Scotland, their headquarters was Torphichen Preceptory near Linlithgow.

During their tenure, they built a fort around the church at Tullich. After they left, a church dating from the early 14th century was built on the site. You can still see one of the arched doorways in the north wall, now blocked up. It was partly rebuilt after the Reformation. Look carefully at the south wall and you might be able to spot two stones with crosses over a door and window. At the time of our visit, the church was barricaded by wire fences – but we could see, through the empty windows, some gravestones sticking out of the muddy ground like prickles on a hedgehog's back. The original floor would have been made of compressed earth, but dry of course, since in those days, it had the luxury of a roof.

The church was still in use until 1789 and served the village, which had the distinction of being the first burgh on Deeside to have its own mercat cross. It held weekly markets and two annual fairs. It declined in the 19th century when Ballater was built, and now all to be seen of it are earthworks to the north-east of the present-day village.

But what is particularly interesting about St Nathalan's is not the ruins of the church but the graveyard, enclosed by an egg-shaped dyke which was rebuilt in the 19th century. The reason for the shape was to present no corner in which the Devil could hide. The recent dead are buried outside the cemetery walls. They will have to beware of the Devil themselves.

Tullich Graveyard

The main attraction in the cemetery is a recently-constructed shelter in which are huddled together a pink granite basin with a drain hole, most probably a font, and fifteen cross-stones of various sizes dating from the 7th to the 9th centuries. They form the largest collection of stones in eastern Scotland, reflecting Tullich's importance in those days. Twenty-seven stones in total have been found on the site.

The star of the collection is a Pictish stone, 5'9" high and 1'9" wide. Its story is a familiar one, at least to me. In 1866, it was discovered by the eagle-eyed Rev. J.G. Michie of Dinnet being used as a window lintel in the church. It bears the usual mysterious symbols associated with Pictish art – the double-disc and Z-rod, a beast, and a mirror. It is reckoned to date from about 700 and, before its use as a lintel, it would appear that it was used as a grave slab, though parts of the carvings were chopped off to make it fit for its new purpose.

It is a dreadful thing to desecrate a grave, but there were other shameful goings-on long after that. Let me fast forward you a thousand years to one wintry day in the 18th century. For some reason, the minister was very late in arriving and, to keep themselves warm, the congregation kept themselves warm by dancing a reel in the kirkyard. Such sinful behaviour on the Sabbath day! The outrage was celebrated in a poem written in 1776 by John Skinner (1721-1807), to the strathspey tune *The Reel of Tullochgorum*. Burns said it was the "best Scotch song I ever saw". Praise indeed from the master lyricist, though I would have thought "heard" would have been more apposite.

In my view, however, something even more shocking took place a century later, in 1857 to be precise. According to the Rev. Michie, aforesaid, St Nathalan's cross – which once stood to the east of the church – was removed and ground up for road metalling. There was just no respect in those days. Any standing stone or any other that formed part of a disused abbey or church was regarded as fair game by the latter-day builders.

Shortly after the cemetery,

The Pass of Ballater

the A93 takes a bend to the south but we take the B972 straight on through the densely-wooded Pass of Ballater. Some people can't see the wood for the trees, but we can't see the cliffs for them. Presently, however, a car park appears off to the right where we make a stop. From there we see the cliffs rising sheer to the skies.

You may remember this is where the Black Colonel is said to have made a daring escape from the Redcoats by riding up the cliff face. Granted, this is the north side, but I have to say if there is any truth in that story, the south side – where he accomplished the feat – would have to be a darned sight less precipitous than this.

Chapter Fifteen

Corgarff: A Very Unlucky Castle

THE A939 is taking us through Glen Gairn. Grantown-on-Spey, journey's end, is a mere thirty-three miles away. The greatest is behind. But maybe not, if it's the scenery you are talking about.

At Torbeg, the road narrows to a single track with passing places, giving us a feeling that we really are leaving civilisation behind, heading into a wilder, remoter sort of Scotland. When we cross the River Gairn at Glenshiel Lodge, we are back on the route of the Old Military Road. We're climbing steadily now through the hills, then suddenly the A939 takes a sudden fork to the left and we come to Corgarff the village, followed shortly afterwards by the brown sign which directs us up the track to the castle.

It's currently in the care of Historic Environment Scotland, and was recently given a makeover. As a result, its whitewashed walls stand out like a beacon from its surroundings in this bleak and practically treeless setting – apart from the recently-planted regiments of soldier pines, that is. You might be forgiven for supposing that in this remote expanse of unpopulated hill and moorland that hardly anything exciting ever happened here, as Eliza Doolittle more-or-less aspirated in *My Fair Lady*. If you did think that, you couldn't have been more wrong.

The castle is thought to have been built by John Forbes of Towie about 1550 – a tower house enclosed by walls. Back then they would have been much simpler: rectangular, not star-shaped, as they are now. The reason for that, I shall come to presently.

The Forbes family were supporters of the infant king James VI who, as you may remember, after his mother's forced abdication, was being brought up in the Protestant faith in Stirling Castle by the 18th Earl of Mar. The Forbes' enemies were the Gordons from Auchindoun Castle near Dufftown who supported his Catholic mother. They weren't exactly close, but they were the neighbours from hell.

In 1571, Adam Gordon tried to capture the castle. The Forbes men were out, probably gone a-hunting to put food on the table. The mistress of the castle refused to surrender and shot one of Gordon's men through the knee with a pistol. This probably annoyed Gordon more than just a little bit – not that that would have made any difference anyway, as he was intent on setting fire to the castle. It was a massacre. He killed them all: women, children, servants – twenty-six in all.

Corgarff Castle

One story tells of how, in an attempt to send for help, they wrapped a small girl in a blanket and threw her out of a garret window. Unfortunately she landed on top of a bayonet. Another version has it that they lowered her by the well-known method of knotting sheets together only for her to be bayonetted when she reached the ground. Struck by her beauty and in a fit of remorse for what he had done, the killer wrote a lament called *Edom o' Gordon*. Her ghost is said to haunt the castle, and visitors to the garret room are reported to have felt an eerie feeling...

In revenge, the Gordons' castle of Auchindoon was burned by William Mackintosh. For his pains, he was arrested and beheaded by the Countess of Huntly's cook. They never told him that that beheading folk was part of the job description, but I suppose he was used to cutting the heads off animals. And not to be outdone in the song stakes, Mackintosh had a ballad written in his honour too – *The Burning of Auchindoon*. By 1594, the castle was back in the hands of the Gordons, but by 1725 it was derelict.

As for Corgarff, in 1607 it was taken over by outlaws for a while and in 1609, another lot of thieves made off with the cattle. In 1626, the castle was acquired by John Erskine, the 2nd Earl of Mar. If you remember (and I don't blame you if you don't), he was one of the Ruthven Raid conspirators who snatched James VI and played pass-the-parcel with him thereafter.

In 1645, it became the mustering point for the troops of James Graham, 1st Marquess of Montrose (1612-50), during the English Civil War. He was fighting for the Stuarts that time. In the First and Second Bishop's Wars in 1639 and 1640 respectively, he had been on the side of the Covenanters *against* the King. It turned out to be a fatal change of side. After his defeat at the Battle of Carbisdale on 27th April 1650, he ended up on the run, supposedly so famished he had to resort to eating one of his gloves. He put himself under the protection of Neil MacLeod of Assynt at Ardveck Castle, only to be betrayed by him and finally ending up at the end of a rope in Edinburgh on 21st May 1650.

In 1689, Corgarff was put to the flames for a second time. This time it was by the "friends" of the castle – the Jacobites – to prevent it falling into the hands of the opposition, William of Orange. Then in 1715, our old friend John Erskine, the 23rd Earl of Mar, aka "Bobbing John", flew the Jacobite flag a second time at Kildrummy and marched his men to Corgarff to collect weapons before marching to Braemar.

He gambled all, and had James VIII been crowned, what a grateful monarch he would most surely have been! As it happened, Mar lost everything. As part of the reprisals, his estates were forfeited and Corgarff was put to the torch for a third time. How unlucky can a castle be? So much for supposing that hardly anything ever happened here! In actual fact, in those turbulent times, it was the equivalent of living on the edge of a tectonic plate.

Fast forward thirty years to 1746 and once again Corgarff was playing a pivotal role in Scottish history. Following Prince Charlie's retreat from Derby, a detachment of Jacobites used Corgarff as an arms store (again). A forced march by the Redcoats, led by Lord Ancrum through the snow from Aberdeen, caught the Jacobites napping. Well, that's not quite true. The only living thing the troops found in the castle was the cat, contentedly napping by the still-burning fire. Somehow the Jacobites got advance warning of the impending attack and, in their precipitate haste to leave, left behind 300 muskets as well as barrels of gunpowder.

Would it have made any difference to the ultimate outcome at Culloden a few months later in April of the same year if they had been brought to the fray? Very likely not. There are very many reasons why the Jacobites were defeated at Culloden and had to retreat to the glens after that fateful day to grieve over the fallen and repent in sorrow.

As part of the measures to snuff out, not just a third rebellion, but Highland culture as a whole, Corgarff was converted into a barracks in 1748. To begin with, it housed a commanding officer, Lieutenant Leslie, three non-commissioned officers and up to forty-two men. Think of Fort

Well at Corgarff Castle

View from Corgarff Castle

George at Ardersier hunkering down behind its massive star-shaped defensive walls and you can see that the new King, William III, was taking no chances. And that's why you see the star-shaped walls here, equipped with musket loops, guarding the tower house, just as we had seen at Braemar Castle. Claymores versus muskets fired from behind stout walls. No contest. You would have to have been mad to attempt it. For the first time in its life, Corgarff could relax, safe in the knowledge that it would never be attacked again.

It continued as a barracks, home for about twenty-five men with the same number sleeping outside the walls – in barns or in homes which they commandeered, just because they could. They were policemen on the lookout for an infringement of the new bans, such as the wearing of the kilt.

And that's how HES presents Corgarff today. Barracks-living, 18th century style. Consider that bed for example. Not the soft mattress, pillow, clean sheets and blankets you are accustomed to in your own little love nest. In fact, that mattress looks rather thin. But it gets worse. Now look at the same bed and imagine that narrow space was not yours alone, and you had to share it and that thin blanket with another soldier whom you didn't even fancy. And I won't even mention the snoring. Who would a soldier be?

A rail above the beds runs round the room on which the soldiers hung their uniforms and equipment, whilst a wooden stand beside the fireplace is where they placed their muskets. In front of it is a table and benches with wooden plates. They are clearly reproductions, but it's interesting to see that in the interests of verisimilitude, the initials RJM have been lovingly carved in cursive script into the top of the table. You know how soldiers like to indulge in a bit of graffiti to whittle away the boredom.

On a whim, I pick up one of the plates and look at the base. I am gratified to find my hunch was right – more carvings. How could those with a penchant for defacing property resist such an inviting and malleable material? One is particularly interesting. It lists the exploits of the 36th Regiment which was founded by William Caulfeild, 2nd Viscount Charlemont in 1701 in Ireland. (Not William, the Road Builder.) As the replica plate with its rude carving testifies, the regiment first saw service in Gibraltar and went on to fight at Falkirk and Culloden, to name the two battles with a Scottish connection. As for the others, most were just content to carve their initials as if to say: "My plate. Hands off."

The officers' apartment on the floor below is a bit more roomy, as you would expect. It served as their office, sitting room and bedroom. The fireplace, with a very much blackened lintel, features a military hob-grate; not the original one, but a contemporary. Shelved cupboards once stood on either side of it. There would also have been some simple furniture to add to the room to make it a little more homely.

At the beginning of the 19th century the castle reverted to being a farmhouse, but the Government requisitioned it again in 1827. This time the enemies were the illegal whisky distillers and smugglers who were rife in the area. For their first victim, the killjoys had to look no further than the castle itself where, in the 1820s, the entrepreneurial farmer James McHardy turned his surplus grain into whisky, mainly for his own consumption. What he couldn't drink himself, he sold to the locals. You can still see a copper still, a stone fireplace, and wooden barrels. Easy to imagine the good Mr McHardy hard at work here producing his home brew.

The army finally left in 1831. The final residents were the Ross sisters, known as the "Castle Ladies", who left during the First World War. The present custodian, as I said above, is Historic Environment Scotland. On the top floor there is a selection of clothes where the kids can indulge their imaginations by dressing up in army uniforms and kilts. Jacobite or Hanoverian? Take your pick.

The star attraction however, on a table at the other end of the room and enclosed in a glass cube, is an impressive reconstruction of the castle as it would have looked in 1746 – made out of about 7,000 Lego bricks. The walls of the castle have been cut away so you can get an idea of what life was like inside. The landscape which surrounds it features the wildlife native to the Cairngorms National Park. It also includes some animals of the domesticated sort. Take a bow, Dan Harris. I am sure you spent as many happy hours making it as those have who have enjoyed looking at it.

At the end of the track that takes us away from the castle, we are back on the Snow Roads proper. And if anywhere could be said to mark where the "snow" part of that route starts, then this is it.

Chapter Sixteen

Over the Lecht: The Postmistress, the Ski Centre and the Well

WE climb steadily upwards until, after a mile or two, we come to the second of the three artists' installations along the route. As well as admiring them for their own sake, they encourage tourists to stop and take in the landscape. Away down there, in its whiteness, the Lilliputian Corgarff Castle is easy to pick out.

The installation is a combined creation called *The Watchers* by John Kennedy and *A Moment in Time* by Louise Gardner. To my eyes, there is something spooky about the rust-coloured, coffin-shaped *Watchers*, where, if you can forget your mortality for a moment, you can take a seat and admire the wide landscape spread out before you. Here you can sit and reflect that long after you are reduced to dust or ashes, those hills will still be here, imperceptibly reduced by inches, not noticeable to the naked eye even a thousand years from now, and aeons before they will be ground down to the dust that you were reduced to so, so long ago.

The other exhibit is earlier and consists of holes bored through a standing stone so when you look through them, it's as if looking through a telescope at the scene at the other end, except it is the same

A Moment in Time

size as it was before. On each of its four faces is carved, in block capitals:

TAKE A MOMENT TO BEHOLD
AS STILL SKIES OR STORMS UNFOLD
IN SUN RAIN SLEET OR SNOW
START YOUR SOUL BEFORE YOU GO

I rather like that. Very poetic. And just as well the stone is made of granite, considering the extremes of the Scottish climate it is exposed to.

I'm not sure how to start my soul but I do know how to start the car and onwards and upwards we go towards Cock Bridge which marks the southerly point of the infamous Cock Bridge to Tomintoul road over the Lecht (from the Gaelic *An Leac* – "the flat rock"). It seems an odd name for such a mountainous area. This road is notorious for being the first in the whole of the UK to be closed by snow in the winter. If you are a betting man, you could put money on it, but don't expect to make your fortune – the bookies are not stupid.

In 1999, after that national treasure, Terry Wogan, criticised Aberdeen Council on Radio 2 for failing to keep the road open, outraged locals were quick to point out that it wasn't the Council's responsibility but that of the Tomintoul postmistress, Mrs MacKay. Year after year, she failed in her task, but – to be fair to her – all she had was a silver-handled shovel (to match her hair) and bless her, she did the best her meagre equipment and advanced years would allow. What a soulless task. And what thanks did she get – just a lot of abuse. Not only that, she had the day job to do as well, handing out pensions, probably to people far younger than her. What did they expect one frail old woman to do against Mother Nature with all her awesome power? No wonder the road became blocked every winter.

The Watchers

You may dismiss this as a bit of mischief-making by Wogan, that Mrs MacKay was more of a myth than a missus. Wrong. Listeners to the show phoned in to say they had seen the good lady at her task as early as June. It pays to start early, but the odds were stacked against her. I have not heard any report of her death so I am assuming global warming must come as a great relief to her. Even so, she must surely be look-

Cock Bridge to Tomintoul Road

ing forward to the day when she can hang up her shovel and concentrate on the day job.

And so we come to Cock Bridge, a scattered community if never I saw one. After we had passed it, or rather assumed we must have, not having seen as much as a sign to it, we come to a lay-by. There we see do see a green sign, which reads: *Old Military Road / Coupar Angus to Fort George / Cockbridge 3 miles.* We have been following the Old Military Road for much of the way since Blairgowrie, and here is a stretch of the original road which gives us an idea of how it might have looked when it was first built in 1752. I follow it with my eyes, an ever-narrowing ribbon wending its way over the bleak moor, far into the distance. It strikes me just what a massive project Caulfeild's was, and just how back-breaking the work of transporting the stone, breaking it up, and laying and bedding it down. And where, pray, was the nearest quarry? Nothing remotely like one that I can see, and I can see for miles and miles.

It looks an inhospitable sort of landscape, but a noticeboard nearby tells us this vast expanse of peat, heather, moss and grasses is home, at different times of the year, to black and red grouse, partridge, ptarmigan, curlew, lapwing, golden plover, golden eagle, snipe, hen harrier and merlin. There are mammals too, such as deer, mountain hares, foxes and stoats. They may well be there, hunkered down in the heather out of sight, but there's not a single sign of any human life or habitation. Turning my gaze back to the present road, the one we are about to resume, it certainly is a lot wider but – as it unwinds towards the hills on the horizon – there is no sign of life there either: not a house nor another car in sight.

Civilisation manifests itself again when we arrive at the *Leac A' Ghobian*, the Lecht Ski Centre, 2,090 feet above sea level. It sits astride the Moray/Aberdeenshire border, which is announced by a sign welcoming the traveller to "Moray – Malt Whisky Country" and below it a brown sign proclaims "Historic Banffshire". It may just be a sign to most people, but it is a sad sign to me – a Banffshire *loon* – a reminder that the county of my birth has been cast into the dustbin of history. In my daily life, I try to put this sad state of affairs to the back of my mind but this sign comes as a bit of a jolt to the memory, not to mention the body, as we rattle over the cattle grid and we cross into the historic past.

The Ski Centre opened in 1977 with three ski tows and a small café in a hut that could seat thirty people. The first chair lift was added in 1999 and, since then, has grown and grown. Not only that; it has also got better and better. In 2004, the hut was replaced with a £1 million lodge with a bar and restaurant.

Lecht Ski Centre

Meanwhile, in the great outdoors, there are slopes to suit all abilities: seven green slopes, seven blue, five red, and one black. Skiers don't need to be told the significance of the colour coding, and everyone knows "black" means bad... except that for skiers of a certain calibre, it means precisely the opposite. The runs are named after local birds, mainly raptors, the exceptions being the gentle Bunting, Robin and Wren.

The Lecht was one of the first to offer instruction in the art of snowboarding. It's a foreign country to me with its own language which includes such esoteric words such as half-pipe, gap-jumps, log-slides and table-tops. Snowboarders, I know, will be impressed... but I am non-plussed.

If nature does not oblige by supplying enough of the white stuff, the Centre can make its own with snow cannons whose sights are trained on five runs. You can imagine what Mrs MacKay thinks of that. I can see her down on her bended knees before she goes to bed, praying that their aim stays true. As if she didn't have enough work to do already.

During the summer, when there is no snow of any kind, you can take your bike smoothly to the top of the mountain, courtesy of the ski lift, and bumpily ride it down.

A little after the Ski Centre, we come to the Well of Lecht. You will need to be vigilant, despite the brown sign pointing to the picnic site of that name. At the well, by the side of the road, a stone marker commemorates the building of the Old Military Road. At some time in the past, it had been broken into two parts across its breadth. It reads:

A****D 1754
FIVE· COMPANES
THE·332· REGMENT·
RIGHT·HONer· LOR

*CHAs· HAY· COLONEL
MADE· THE· ROAD·FROM
HERE·TO· THE
SPEY*

By "Spey" the sculptor actually means Ruthven Barracks but, for reasons of space, rather than laziness, has spared the chisel. The stone is rather narrow and rather ingeniously, the anonymous author has ingeniously combined some letters to save more space. For example, in "COMPANES", the last downstroke of the "M" also forms the downstroke of the "P". But more cunningly, wherever "THE" occurs, the "H" is formed by running a bar between the downstroke of the "T" and the back of the "E". Even where he had room to space the letters out in the penultimate line, the chiseler continued to use the abbreviated form. He must have liked it, and so do I.

The Well of Lecht

Across the road from the well, a short track leads to a car park. It is the best place, indeed the *only* place to stop, if you want to have a closer look at the well. You can also see a building in the distance, hemmed in by hills. It's only half-a-mile to get there, as you follow the banks of the burn.

The building in the distance is what is left of a manganese ore crushing mill which was powered by a massive 26 foot-diameter waterwheel set in one of the gable-end walls. It was given a new roof in the 1980s by Moray Council. Also to be seen are the remains of the lade, spoil heaps, and some of the mine workings, dug into the hillside.

It began in 1730 as an iron ore mine operated by the York Buildings Company of London. The ore was taken across the hills by ponies to Coulnakyle near Nethy Bridge, five miles to the south of Grantown. Who would a pony be? The smelting furnaces were fired by trees from Abernethy Forest. Seven years later, the trees were given a reprieve when the mine incurred heavy losses and shut down.

It was resurrected in 1841 by the Duke of Richmond and Gordon as a manganese mine, employing 60 men and boys. The ore was sent to Newcastle for use in the bleach trade. At the time, it was the largest manganese mine in Scotland and has not been surpassed to this day. Truth to tell, it didn't fare any better than the iron mine. It lasted only five years because of cheaper ore being imported from Russia.

If you fancy a longer walk, and you have the time (which we don't), you can take the public path to Chapeltown via Scalan Seminary. The green sign says it is 6km and, beneath it, a noticeboard imparts the information that between the 1780s and the 1830s, this path was one of the many "Whisky Roads" that smugglers used to transport their illicit goods from the hidden stills in the hills to consumers in the cities to the south and east.

The seminary was also illicit, tucked away amongst the hills. We'll be going to it later, but in the meantime, you will get an

Smugglers' Path to Manganese Mine at Well of Lecht

idea of just how remote this place is when I tell you that the car park is one of the Dark Skies Discovery Sites, the so-called "Field of Hope". The velvet dark is pricked with a myriad of stars including the Milky Way which contains an estimated 100 to 400 billion stars and has a diameter of between 150,000 and 200,000 light years. Since light travels at the awesome speed of 671,000,000 mph, the fastest thing in the universe – apart from the hypothetical tachyon (don't ask me – ask Einstein) – it gives you an idea of just how mind-bogglingly vast it is.

Marvel and feel humbled at the immensity of the universe and reflect how extraordinarily arrogant it would be for us to assume that our fragile little planet on the edge of our galaxy was the only one to support life, even if it is not as we know it, Jim. And surely, out of an estimated two trillion galaxies (and that's just in the observable universe), you would think that the odds must be in favour of there being at least one star with a planet that resembles Earth – if not its identical twin. As Carl Sagan memorably wrote in his *Cosmos* (1980): "the number of stars in the universe is greater than all the grains of sand on all the beaches of the planet Earth". Astronomers now think that's actually something of an underestimation.

Perhaps, when we die, all will be revealed. Peter Pan thought to do so would be "an awfully big adventure". I hope he is right. If he is wrong, death is going to be incredibly dull.

Chapter Seventeen

Tomintoul: The Laird, the Swindler and the Mutineer

TOMINTOUL. Visitors, please note: the last syllable is pronounced by the locals to sound like something we use to dry ourselves. People who don't know any better pronounce it like something used to facilitate a task.

It is often alleged that Tomintoul is the highest village in Scotland. This undoubtedly stems from the supposition that you would expect to find it in the Highlands, whereas in actual fact, the honour belongs to Wanlockead in the Southern Uplands. Not only that, but Dalwhinnie, on the A9, is also a few feet higher than Tomintoul.

However true that may, Tomintoul has more of a look of a town to it than a village, and it certainly looks much more urbanised than either of its rivals. The dictionary unhelpfully defines "town" as a "densely populated urban area, bigger than a village and smaller than a city". To use the analogy of the proverbial waterfowl, I would argue that if it looks like a duck, walks like a duck, and quacks like a duck, then it probably *is* a duck. I am happy therefore to say I have arrived in the highest town in Scotland, even if the population barely breaks into the seven hundreds once the tourists have drifted away like melting snow – the very stuff that brought them to stay here whilst enjoying the ski slopes at the Lecht only five miles away.

Its name comes from the Scots Gaelic *Tom an t-sabhail*, meaning "hillock of the barn". Back in the beginning, there were settlements in the area, but Tomintoul the village, as it was then, did not exist until 1775. In the aftermath of the failed Jacobite Rebellions, that jolly good bloke and lenient laird, Alexander, 4th Duke of Gordon (1743-1827), aka the "Cock o' the North" (the traditional name given to the head of that clan), decided to create a new village to improve the lives of his displaced tenants. Naturally, he was canny enough to build it on the Old Military Road, today's A939. It also lies at the junction of several old drove roads to which the cattle were driven to market. Nearby was a peat bog and woods for firewood, and limestone to reduce the acidity of the soil.

The Duke's master plan was to grow flax and build a mill to process it into linen. Alas, the ground was too poor for flax to thrive and the mill was never built. Instead, the first settlers were reduced to having to scrape a living from keeping a few cattle, cultivating small plots of land which were too small to sustain them, and picking up casual work whenever they could. He also had another plan, or motive, which was to curb the reiving which was rife in the area and put an end to the number of illicit stills, estimated to number about 200.

As a matter of fact, Tomintoul was only one of three villages he founded. Fochabers, the place of his birth (actually in Gordon Castle near there), was the first in 1776, and Portgordon followed in 1797.

Alexander came to the Dukedom when he was only nine, and he went on to become a Scottish representative peer in 1767 and a Knight of the Thistle in 1775. He was twice Keeper of the Great Seal of Scotland from 1794-1804 and from 1807 until his death twenty years later.

In 1794, he also founded the 100th (Gordon Highlanders) Regiment of Foot, later renamed the 92nd, as a response to the threat posed by Revolutionary France. His wife, the Duchess, Jane Maxwell, did her bit for the cause, placing the "king's shilling" between her lips and thus each new recruit was also rewarded with a kiss. She probably kissed a good few other men in her time, for she was a celebrated beauty and a socialite in London. Meanwhile, the Duke stayed in seclusion in Gordon Castle. By the time of her death in 1812, they were bitterly estranged. All the same, in happier times, they managed to produce seven children together.

In 1820, when he was 77, the Duke married Jane (or Jean) Christie, aged about 40, by whom he had already had four children. Evidently, when it comes to marriage and making babies, it isn't just the present generation who put the cart before the horse, so to speak. Incidentally, his younger brother, George, was responsible for inciting the Gordon riots of 1780, which, lest you have forgotten, was a protest against the Papists Act of 1778 which gave Catholics a limited amount of emancipation. He died of typhoid fever in Newgate prison in 1793, aged 42.

The Square, Tomintoul

The present town is pretty much as it was in the founder's day, laid out in a grid pattern, with a 40-foot wide main street and a grass square in the middle. The drinking fountain was added in 1915. Queen Victoria visited in 1860 and did not give it a good write-up in her journal. She wrote: "*Tomintoul is the most tumble-down, poor-looking place I ever saw – a long street with three inns, miserable dirty-looking houses and people, and a sad look of wretchedness about it.*" I think it's fair to conclude she was not impressed. Pity she can't come back and see it today: neat and tidy, prosperous-looking.

Tomintoul and Glenlivet Discovery Centre

We begin our exploration at the Tomintoul and Glenlivet Discovery Centre, which lies at one end of the grassy square. After cash-strapped Moray Council withdrew funding in 2014, thanks to a cash injection from the Heritage Lottery Fund and Cairngorms LEADER (a French acronym: *Liaison Entre Actions de Développement de l'Economie Rurale,* a EU initiative to support rural development), it re-opened in 2018 and is operated by the Tomintoul & Glenlivet Development Trust. It provides historical records, oral history recordings and objects such as a 4,000-year-old flint arrowhead and a scraper for cleaning animal hides. Arguably, the star of the museum is the Tomintoul Coat.

Similar to a WWI army trench coat, only with eight mother-of-pearl buttons instead of standard army issue, it was found stuffed between the rafters in an attic. It is thought to date from the early 19th century and probably belonged to an exciseman – but who he was and why the coat was hidden away, sadly no-one knows, and it's unlikely we shall ever find out. Still, as I said earlier, the mystery is part of the attraction; perhaps even the greater part.

Take particular note of the Gordon Arms Hotel which dominates the square. It was once in the ownership of Tony Williams, aka the "Laird of Tomintoul". He discovered Tomintoul while on holiday in Ballater and fell in love with it. To the residents of his adopted town, he styled himself "Lord Williams", giving them the impression that his vast wealth was due to his being an aristocrat. In actual fact he was a crook, which is not necessarily a contradiction in terms.

In his working life, he had been Deputy Director of Finance for the Metropolitan Police and, over a period of twelve years, defrauded it of £5.3 million.

That shows a certain degree of cunning, not to mention a certain amount of cheek. It all began in 1981 with the theft of £200 from a benevolent fund, and when no-one noticed, he carried on finding himself in financial difficulties after the break-up of his first marriage. A break of another kind came when he was appointed in sole control of a secret fund that had been set up to conduct undercover surveillance of the IRA and pay informers.

In the 1990s, he set up a company, "Tomintoul Enterprises Ltd.", and set about buying up and improving the town. His first purchase was a cottage on the Square. He went on to buy and spend £1.5m on refurbishing the Gordon Arms, bought more cottages, a pub, a tearoom and the Clockhouse restaurant on which he spent a cool £500,000 on refurbishments. He also bought a timeshare at the nearby Craigendarroch Country Club which boasts, amongst its members, the Royal Family. Splash the cash and act like an aristocrat. No wonder he fooled everyone.

Like other exceptionally wealthy people, he banked with Coutts, bankers to the Queen. He also had bank accounts in London, Scotland, and the Channel Islands. Furthermore, he had two houses, mansions actually, in Surrey, as well as a flat in Westminster. He also rented another in Mayfair at £2,000 a month, not to mention the little matter of a villa on the Costa del Sol. And here's the thing – all this on a salary of £42,000! He told his wife, Kay, he had inherited a fortune from a rich uncle in Norway and, willingly, she believed. One should always choose one's uncles carefully and if he doesn't exist, it may be necessary to invent him, as Voltaire famously said about God.

When he first began spending freely in Tomintoul, the residents could hardly believe their luck. To them, Williams must have seemed like an angel, providing employment for around forty people. That's a significant number out of such a small population. But as the old dictum has it: *if it's too good to be true, then it probably is.* And perhaps being called the "laird" went to his head because he started buying up aristocratic titles, nine Scottish titles in all, as well as the 15th century Barony of Chirnside in Berwickshire, which is how he managed to get rid of another £80,000.

The Clockhouse, Tomintoul

Sadly, it all ended in tears when his *pochling* was discovered. His banks had become suspicious because his deposits were so enormous they suspected something fishy and brought the matter to the attention of the police. In May 1995, he was sentenced in the Old Bailey to seven-and-a-half years at Her Majesty's pleasure. His assets were frozen and the Barony of Chirnside was put up for auction, but only around £750,000 of the millions he had stolen were recovered. He was released in 1999 and worked as a bus driver as part of a prison-release scheme. Tomintoul's benefactor was, of course, no danger to the public. He was a gentleman crook.

The owner of the now-defunct Tomintoul Brewery, Andrew Neame, brought out a beer called *The Laird of Tomintoul* with a label in the shape of a metropolitan policeman's helmet. A local woodcarver, Donald Corr, who wrote a verse account of Williams' doings, said this of the ale:

"The Laird of Tomintoul", it's called,
And it's newly out on bail.
Although it's slightly bitter
(Like many folk up here)
You'll like "The Laird of Tomintoul"
An honest, wholesome beer.

Cor, blimey! All I can say is don't give up the day job, Mr Corr.

If this caper sounds to you like the sort of film that might have come from the Ealing Studios, you wouldn't be far wrong. Phoenix Pictures planned to make a film of these events called *The Laird* but, after two years, talks stalled between the company and the director, Mel Smith. There was also the difficulty of Williamson benefiting from his crimes.

One film, or rather a BBC TV series, that *was* made with a Tomintoul connection was *The Monocled Mutineer* (1986). Billed as a "true-life story", it told the story of Francis Percy Toplis (1896-1920), who served as a private in the Royal Army Medical Corps as a stretcher-bearer. The "Mutineer" part of the title refers to Toplis's alleged involvement in the Étaples Mutiny from 9th-12th September 1917. As I mentioned earlier, the things you see in the theatre need to be taken with a pinch of salt, to put it mildly, and the same applies to TV films. According to the film, Toplis played a leading part in the mutiny – a protest about a brutal training regime – whereas in actual fact, there is no evidence that he was even there. Indeed, his unit was on board the *Orantes* on its way to India at the time, and there is no indication to suggest that he was not on board.

Toplis had a bit of a past. Before the war, in 1912, he was sentenced to two years' hard labour for the attempted rape of a 15-year-old girl. After the war, he served two years in prison for fraud. On his release, he joined the Royal Army Service Corps where he got up to his old tricks again, selling rationed fuel on the black market – to name just one dodgy act. It was during this time that, when off-duty and to impress the ladies, he dressed up as a colonel wearing a gold monocle.

On 20th April 1920, he allegedly murdered a taxi driver, Sidney George Spicer, near Andover. He was tried in his absence and found guilty, the first time this had happened in British legal history. He went on the run, hiding in London and adopting the persona aforesaid.

The hue and cry in the press and the huge police effort involved in trying to track him down forced Toplis to flee. He ended up in a bothy on the Glenlivet estate at Badnafrave on the Lecht road. His undoing came when he used some fence posts to light a fire. The smoke was seen by the gamekeeper, John Mackenzie. Since the bothy should have been uninhabited, he informed George Greig, the bobby from Tomintoul. Accompanied by the farmer, John Grant, they set off to investigate. They found a man asleep on the kitchen floor. He was allowed to dress in the bedroom which he did, but returned with a revolver in his hand. He shot Greig in the shoulder and Grant in the thigh before making his escape on a bicycle which fortunately, for him, he had recently had repaired in Tomintoul. He pedalled to Aberdeen, sixty miles away – no little distance, and not all on the flat either by any means. At Aberdeen, he boarded a train to Carlisle.

Five days later, on 6th June, he was spotted, partly-dressed in army uniform, on the Carlisle to Penrith road by PC Alfred Fulton who challenged him. Toplis drew his revolver, but Fulton somehow managed to escape. He returned with armed reinforcements to find Toplis walking down the road heading towards Plumpton. When accosted, Toplis turned to flee, firing at the three police officers as he did so. They returned the fire. One shot was fatal.

Three days later, he was buried in Beacon Edge Cemetery in Penrith in an unmarked grave. Only the gravedigger, two senior police officers, a member of the Board of Guardians (a charitable

Cottage in Tomintoul

organisation who had paid for the funeral), and the vicar were in attendance.

The previous day, an inquest returned the verdict that "Toplis was justifiably killed by a revolver bullet fired by a police officer in the execution of his duty". It also recommended that all three officers should be honoured for their courageous action. Who actually fired the fatal shot is not known for certain.

Yet another film – a comedy drama, *One Last Chance* – was filmed in and around Tomintoul in 2004. It concerns the attempts of three young men to break the bonds of small-town life and go to the city, as so many of their peers had done before them.

It's all a load of hokum. What isn't, is that in the 18th century, in Tomintoul, there lived a man called Grigor Willox. He was reputed to be a white witch; that is to say, someone who used his magical powers for benevolent purposes. He supposedly made dry cows produce milk and barren women produce children. He apparently was also able to detect thieves and break the spells of wicked witches. A very useful person to have around. A real pillar of the community.

The tools of his trade, the secret of his mysterious powers, was a brass hook from a kelpie's bridle and a mermaid's stone made of pure crystal. A kelpie, from the Gaelic *calpa* or *cailpeach*, meaning a "heifer" or "colt", is a water sprite which takes the form of a horse, but – from time to time – can appear in human form. They sometimes come tacked up with a bridle, and sometimes also saddled. When they appear in human form, they are said to retain their hooves, giving them an association with the Devil. Burns makes such a reference in his *Address to the Deil* (1786). And by the way, should one appear in front of you already tacked up, don't whatever you do, mount it, because it will bear you off to its watery home and you will be drowned.

Willox supposedly acquired the bridle part from his ancestor, James MacGrigor, who managed to steal it from the legendary kelpie of Loch Ness – which is not to be confused in any shape or form with the monster of that ilk that also dwells in those murky waters. The trophy was passed down through the generations and came to be known as "Willox's Ball and Bridle".

I have no idea how he came by the mermaid's crystal, but I *can* tell you he used to immerse the crystal in water and sell the infusion as a health cure for 1/6 a shot. It's only a rough estimation, but that's about £8 a bottle in today's money. He travelled all over the Highlands performing his good deeds and making a killing at the same time. But you can't put too high a price on your health and a miracle cure, can you?

Another celebrated resident was Mrs Jean McKenzie who, according to Rev. John Grant, writing in 1791, tells us she kept the best inn in Tomintoul. She had kept a similar establishment in Grantown, but which she left under bit of a cloud. Her career began in 1745, when aged only fourteen, and with an "accommodating disposition of an easy virtue", she was with a regiment in Flanders, "caressing and caressed". Later, she married and set sail for America in search of adventure "in the fields of Venus or Mars, as occasion offered". After a "variety of vicissitudes in Germany, France, Holland, England, Ireland, Scotland, America and the West Indies", life in Tomintoul must have seemed rather tame.

Mrs MacKay, the postmistress, we have already mentioned. By contrast, her life seems far less exciting and much more one of hard toil. Who would you rather be – in the winter months especially?

Chapter Eighteen

Glenlivet: Two Distilleries and a Seminary

AS most people know, Tomintoul lies at the end (or the beginning) of the Whisky Trail. No kidding; there are as many as twenty-five distilleries within a twenty-mile radius of the town. That makes it sound like some other Mecca to me. However, before we we set off up the world-famous Glenlivet (possibly from the Gaelic *liobhaite*, meaning "slippery or smooth place" – or it might come from early or pre-Gaelic word meaning "full of water"), we are going to visit somewhere else first – Craig Haulkie Quarry, which lies on the A939 a mile or so out of town to the north.

This was a source of the stones for the military road that General Caulfeild made, the one we have largely been following on this trip. Also of interest, a path to the side of the quarry leads to the last of the three Snow Roads art installations – *Still* by Angus Richie and Donald Tyler. It is a place for reflection in more ways than one. It consists of a cube open to the front and the rear with polished sides in which are reflected the Cairngorms and the River Avon. You can sit in the cube and be reflected as your mind reflects on the meaning of life, or anything else you care to, as you gaze at the gentle rolling landscape before your eyes.

Back in town, and before setting out on the B9008 to Glenlivet, as a sort of aperitif, we visit The Whisky Castle on the High Street, a veritable Aladdin's cave of malt whiskies if ever I saw one. It's almost enough to make you

Craig Haulkie Quarry

Still Art Installation

think you must have died and gone to heaven.

This amazing place has been operating from the same premises for more than a century and what the owners don't know about malt whisky isn't worth knowing. There are more than 600 to choose from, many of them single cask and rare editions. But where do you begin? Impossible to sample all of the varieties on offer and, in any case, after a few you couldn't trust your tastebuds to distinguish between the subtler tones. Fortunately The Whisky Castle offers free tastings, but you have to book first.

In the 18th and 19th centuries, there were about 200 illegal stills in the glen of the Livet. It was, in fact, a home industry to which many turned a blind eye – even some excisemen. You can walk some of the smugglers' trails today, like the one at the Well of Lecht, as they wend their way through the hills and far away to consumers in Aberdeen, Perth and Edinburgh. The smugglers needed to be constantly on the alert for the excisemen. Very often, the hooves of the ponies which carried the casks of whisky were muffled with straw.

In 1823, the Duke of Gordon, at his factor's suggestion, granted George Smith – a farmer on the estate – some money to start up a legal business at Drumin. Smith registered his product as "The Glenlivet", and that is the name it still bears today. It was not a popular move amongst his former smuggling pals, who hoped in vain that the Licensing Act of 1823 would be repealed. The laird allegedly armed Smith with with a brace of pistols after threats were made on his life. When the distillery at Drumin was destroyed by fire (I wonder how that happened), he built a larger one at Minmore the following year and that is where the whisky is produced to this very day.

The Whisky Castle

After the founding father

went on to found a great distillery in the sky in 1871, his son, John Gordon Smith, inherited. Look at the label on the bottle and you will see it bears their names, George & J. G. Smith. The distillery is presently owned by Pernod Ricard which is as French as frogs' legs. In 2010, it was extended to increase its capacity by 75%. Since 1978, *The Glenlivet* has been the best-selling single malt in the United States – a remarkable achievement. It is hard enough to get to number one in the first place, but to continue to hold the position for more than forty years is quite extraordinary.

Braeval Distillery

We take the B9008 out of town, and after Auchnarrow we take the narrow, sometimes single-track road towards Chapeltown. Presently we find ourselves at Braeval Distillery which, at 1,163 feet, is the highest distillery in Scotland, beating Dalwhinnie by a slender nine feet. It's the new kid on the block, only coming into existence in 1973. In 1994, it changed its name to "Braeval" from "Braes of Glenlivet" to avoid confusion with its illustrious neighbour above. The present owners are Chivas Regal, part of the Pernod Ricard group who bought it from Seagrams in 2001.

Now be prepared to be amazed. The distillery is fully automated! Well, nearly. One man operates the entire operation. No malting is done on the premises, although it flatters to deceive the passer-by with its traditional pagoda roof. A distillery just wouldn't look like one without it. There is nothing to see here: no visitor centre, no warehouses and no bottling plant. To be honest, you're not missing much. Watching whisky being distilled is a bit like watching paint dry. And for your information, bottles of single malt Braeval are extremely rare. Its production of 4 million litres of spirit mainly goes into the making of blends, most of it destined for the Chivas Regal brand. If you are desperate to track down a bottle, The Whisky Castle might be able to help you. If they can't, then I don't know who can. And should you be lucky enough to find one, you will need deep pockets – and what's more, you will need to delve deeply into them.

As you probably know, *uisgue beatha* is the Scots Gaelic for "water of life", which gives us the English word "whisky" and, just after the distillery, we come across another source of that life-sustaining liquid – not another distillery, but a distribution centre for Highland Spring water.

Highland Spring distribution centre

Carrying on past that, we arrive at the Carrachs car park. It's another of the Dark Skies Discovery sites and, from here, a track leads to the Scalan Seminary about a mile away. That is what we have come to see and, to my surprise, we meet a man and his dog. It's only natural, when you meet strangers in remote places like this, to strike up a conversation, and my fellow traveller – pointing to the Ladder Hills climbing out of the moor nearby – unashamedly tells our new acquaintance that about a half-a-century ago she roamed them in her occupation as a grouse-beater. Indeed, so near are they that with the naked eye, we can make out the butts to which she drove the unfortunate birds towards their deaths.

"'Been a bad year for grouse," the old-timer vouchsafes. "No shootin' on the hills this year."

I wittily reply that the grouse would consider that a good year, then we say our farewells and set off to walk down the track. Presently, the whitewashed House of Scalan reveals itself in the distance, nestling at the foot of the hills. Its name comes from the Gaelic *galan*, meaning a turf-roofed shieling or shelter. It was the second seminary in Scotland, the first being on Eilean Ban, an island on Loch Morar. It was destroyed in 1716 in the aftermath of the 1715 Rebellion. This remote part of the Glenlivet estate, under the protective wing of the Catholic Duke of Gordon, seemed an ideal place for its successor, for the turning of boys into priests without them having to travel all the way to Rome to follow their vocation.

The Ladder Hills

The first seminary, mainly made of turf, was founded by Bishop James Gordon with the first boys being recorded there in 1717, despite the date on the sign which puts it at a year earlier. It may have been remote, but it was no secret from the Government troops who caused it some grief, more or less every year, but more seriously in 1726 and twice in 1728.

Scalan Seminary

The present house of stone was built in 1767 by Bishop John Geddes (1735-99), on the other side of the Crombie Burn. It was enlarged in 1738, but more or less razed to the ground in 1746 following the Jacobite defeat at Culloden. It was rebuilt in 1788, bigger and better, most notably with the addition of another storey. After the Catholic Relief Act of 1793 repealed many of the former penal laws, Catholicism was able to emerge from the shadows and the seminary moved to Aquhorthies near Inverurie. A chapel, now in ruins, was tacked onto the north wing of the old seminary to serve the faithful followers of the Old Religion who dwelt amongst the Braes.

During its existence as a seminary, sixty-four "heather priests", as they were called, were nurtured in this nursery. Tom Brown would have thought his schooldays a bit of a doddle compared to theirs. The boys got up at 5am in the summer and 6am in the winter, beginning the day with a bracing bathe in the waters of the Crombie Burn to wash away the cobwebs of sleep. They were given fifteen minutes to do that and dress in their uniform of black and blue tartan before prayer-time. This was followed by meditation for half-an-hour and then it was time for Mass. The fun they had!

The old chapel at Scalan Seminary

At 8am, they sat down to a breakfast of wholesome porridge. Then it was time for studies until lunch at noon. This was followed by an hour's recreation (exercises on the banks of the burn) before it was back to lessons until suppertime and more delicious porridge. A Roman schoolboy would not have been unfamiliar with this regime of *mens sana in corpore sano* which was devised by their founder, Bishop Gordon. After supper, there was more time off before evening prayers when the subject of the next morning's meditation was given out. Bedtime was at 10pm and 9pm in the winter. It wasn't all bad, mind you: they had a treat of meat two or three times a week.

How bleak and drear and cold it must have been in winter! And do not let us forget that at this elevation, even at the height of a Scottish summer, temperatures would have been far from tropical.

Some time after it closed in 1799, Scalan was converted into a farm. A short distance away, on the banks of the burn, are two mill buildings dating from the late 19th and early 20th centuries. Both still retain their waterwheels and threshing machines. Interestingly, they also contain graffiti which give brief insights into life during the post-seminary period. Thus yesterday's vandalism becomes today's historical document. The mills are undergoing restoration and are not open to the public in the meantime.

The seminary, however, is open to the public throughout the year. It is under the care of the Scalan Association, who initially saved the building from collapse and then subsequently set about restoring it. On the ground floor, in the centre of the building, is Bishop Geddes's Room which was later converted into the library. Geddes was here from 1762 to 1767 and elevated to a bishop in 1780. He returned to Scalan in 1793 whilst in poor health, too poorly to take the Mass – though like a "creakin' gate", as the Scots simile has it, he hung on to the mortal coil for another six years.

To the left is "The Big Room", where guests and visitors were made welcome. After Bishop Hay (1729-1811), became Superior at Scalan between 1788 and 1793, the room became known as "Bishop Hay's Room". His box-bed was in the alcove with a curtain in front of it for privacy and cosiness. At the time of his tenure, the boys were expected to master a range of languages: Latin, Greek, French and Hebrew, as well as Geography, Chronology and Rhetoric. It was an education that was second to none.

The boys slept in the attic which had two small windows in the south gable wall and another which faced west. The Superior's living room and bed was at the top of the stairs directly above the previous living room and divided from the dormitory by a wall. It was in this room that in

Mill at Scalan Seminary

1783, the Superior, John Paterson, died probably of tuberculosis, aged only in his early thirties. His coffin had to be lowered through one of the small windows as it was impossible to negotiate it round the corner of the passage and down the stairs.

On the same floor, the chapel lay at the other side of the Superior's room, the altar being at the gable end. From 1767 to 1788, it was also used by the people of the Braes. Access was gained by an outside stair and a window was converted into a door. When the new chapel was built on the north side, the chapel became an oratory for the residents, the stair was removed, and the door became a window again.

So that was Scalan. So many ghosts there and, spookily, as I take my leave, like a scene from *The Birds*, I see that the leafless branches of a nearby tree are festooned with birds – judging from their size, either rooks or ravens. They are too many to count, but there could be sixty-four or more. They are said to portend death, and mock me if you like, but could they possibly be the souls of the boys who would be priests?

By the time my companion joins me, they have, like Peter and Paul in the nursery rhyme, all flown away. She didn't see them, but I know I did.

Chapter Nineteen

Glenlivet: Castles and Battles

AS we head back to the B9008, we have to stop in a passing place to let a tanker go by. Unless I am much mistaken, it is heading for the distillery where its stainless steel tank will be filled with thousands of gallons of the clear white spirit that, three years from now, minimum, will morph into whisky. Better quality takes quite a bit longer. I know not where the tanker will be bound after that, but it occurs to me to wonder if it is given a police escort. It seems an elementary precaution to me, but what do I know?

Our next destination is Blairfindy Castle, tucked away behind the Glenlivet Distillery – though of course it was there a long, long, time before that was built. However, before we come to it and the castle, we come across an unexpected attraction. You could rightly call it "serendipitous" – and, even better, there is a small car park where we can stop to see it better.

It is the Old Bridge of Livet which originally consisted of three arches, but misfortune, in the shape of the *Muckle Spate* of 1829, carried one away. Its construction has erroneously been attributed to General Wade. Never, in the field of road and bridge building, have so many been attributed to one who built so few compared to Caulfeild who built so many more. As a matter of fact, neither of them built this one. It is thought to date from at least a century-and-a-half later than them, and had something to to do with Blairfindy Castle.

It is a very impressive sight with its remaining twin arches looking as high as the humps on a Bactrian camel. Once upon a time the road would have been cobbled but the stones have very much

The Old Bridge of Livet

been covered with vegetation. Meanwhile, underneath the arches, the Livet, brown and frothy, carries on regardless, just as it has done since time immemorial.

We are advised not to walk over the bridge but, seen from the bank, the stones of the arch look more than capable of supporting a little fatty like me. I have no fear of it suddenly collapsing under my weight, but wading through the

The Glenlivet Distillery

wet, waist-high grass is a sufficient deterrent. It would be a far, far better thing to prevent this remarkable bridge from collapse if they removed the weight of all that stuff growing on it. I suppose it all comes down to money – or rather the lack of it.

If I may not walk across the bridge, I can at least admire it from a distance. It's quite remarkable, it really is – so steep the climb up, so steep the descent down, only to have to repeat the whole process again when you come to the second hump.

Carrying on, we come to the Glenlivet Distillery. I stop to take some photos of the source of one of my favourite malts. The air is redolent with a delicious scent. I inhale deep lungfuls of it, and I wonder if those who work there are not perpetually light-headed.

"What a stink!"

This from my companion who has remained in the car whilst I have been on my mission. Stink indeed! If this tells you much about my wife's unsophisticated and uncultured sense of smell, it also tells you how strong the aroma is since she has remained cocooned in the car with the doors closed and the windows firmly up. I wish there was a way of bottling it.

It's only a short drive along the road that bisects the distillery before we get our first glimpse of Blairfindy Castle. And what a disappointment it is! It is clad from top to toe in scaffolding like a medieval knight clad in armour, making it impossible to see the castle apart from getting an impression of its shape. To make matters worse, it's very difficult to get an uninterrupted view because it is tucked in behind by a row of houses. The best place to see it is down the drive of the first house in the row, but a notice written in big black letters that it is impossible to ignore says: THIS IS NOT A VIEWING POINT FOR THE CASTLE.

Out of respect, I drive on past it, just a little way, and although it's awkward to take a photo through the links of the fence which the builders have erected, I really am glad I did, for a moment later, as I am taking photographs as best I can, from around the corner, a man exercising his dog hies into view, and – passing us without a word – turns into the drive. Phew!

The castle was built in 1564 by John Gordon as an L-shaped tower house with a single round turret. In 1586, it passed into the possession of another branch of the family, the Earls of Huntly, who used it as a hunting lodge. Above the arched doorway is the Gordon coat of arms and the initials IG and HG. There is also a box machicolation, or *bretache*, through which nasty things could be thrown down on the heads of attackers, though it is thought that here it was mainly just for decoration. Well maybe it was, but there is a shot-hole to the left-hand side where pot shots could be taken at undesirables.

On the 3rd October 1595, three miles to the north-east of here, George Gordon, the 6th Earl of Huntly, and once a favourite of James VI, along with Francis Hay, 9th Earl of Errol, ambushed the Protestant forces of Archibald Campbell, 7th Earl of Argyll. Argyll's army (which consisted of a confederation of more clans than you could shake a claymore at), despite being vastly more numerous, was routed. Unreliable figures suggest that Huntly and Hay only lost 14 men (it seems a very precise number, as well as a low one), compared to 500 of Argyll's men.

There were several reasons for such a massive defeat. Firstly, it is alleged that John Grant of Gartenberg made a secret deal with Huntly, and the Grants deserted before battle was joined. Then there was the element of surprise, but Huntly would claim he had a better weapon than that – he had God on his side.

Blairfindy Castle

Before the battle, Mass was said, confessions were heard, the weapons were sprinkled with holy water and a white cross was painted on their armour. No wonder Huntly was supremely confident of victory.

But there was was something else. He had 100 cavalry and six cannon – said to be the first time they were used in a battle in Scotland. In another claim to fame, the Battle of Glenlivet, as it is variously named, has the honour of being the highest battleground in the UK. Should you wish to visit it, park at the Forestry

Commission car park at Morinsh on the B9009.

It turned out to be a bit of a Pyrrhic victory for Gordon and Hay. In retribution, Huntly's castle was attacked, Errol's castle was destroyed and both rebels went into exile. However, after renouncing Catholicism and signing a confession of faith on 26th June 1597 in the Auld Kirk in Aberdeen, they were allowed to legally reside in Scotland again and Huntly was restored to James VI's favour, as were his estates. At the baptism of Princess Margaret in 1599, the King created him a marquess. A bit of a turnaround in fortune, you could say.

Half-a-century later, a different King (Charles I), different times, and the English Civil Wars (1642-51), and Blairfindy served as a prison in 1647 when George Gordon, 2nd Marquess of Huntly, was captured at Delnabo near Tomintoul and was kept here for safe-keeping prior to his trial and execution in Edinburgh. His crime was to be a Catholic and a royalist. A multiple offender.

The end for Blairfindy came in 1746 when, after Culloden, it was put to the torch and subsequently abandoned. The restoration works look as if they will take some time.

Retracing our steps through the distillery,f I take the chance to inhale once again the heavenly scent, then we join the B9136 to Drumin Castle. It's hardly any distance.

There is a car park by the river and a flight of fairly-steep wooden steps takes us through the trees to the old walled kitchen garden, while a path to the left leads by a more circuitous route to the castle. There is wheelchair access by another route, and also the two-mile circular Drumin Path along the riverbank and through a wood of old Scots pine and other trees. From here you can also join the trail of that reformed smuggler, George Smith.

The walled garden has been turned into Glenlivet Community Orchard, and in that orchard is a moss-covered bench. It adds enormously to the atmosphere of the place, but looks too fragile to plonk one's posterior on. It should really have a notice on it, or some prickly object like you see in stately homes to prevent you from doing so. Seen from the bench and over the wall of the orchard, the walls of the castle appear to have had a chunk taken out of them like a bite from an apple, appropriately enough.

Drumin Castle from the Community Orchard

It's not certain when the castle was built,

Drumin Castle

but we do know that on the 13th of July 1372, Robert II granted the lands of Strathavon (which included Drumin), to his son, Alexander Stewart (1342-1406) aka the notorious Wolf of Badenoch, and it's most likely the castle was built shortly afterwards. It occupies an imposing and strategic position, probably on the site of an Iron Age Dun, overlooking the confluence of the Livet and the Avon (*A'an* in Gaelic, meaning "very bright one"). According to legend, it was named after Athfhinn, the wife of the Celtic warrior Fionn who was drowned while attempting to cross the river.

In 1490, the Wolf's grandson, Sir Walter Stewart, sold the castle and lands to Alexander, the 3rd Earl of Huntly, although the Stewarts continued to live happily there as tenants until the early 18th century when Charles Stewart was the last-known resident. After that it fell into disuse and, in 1818, it provided a very handy quarry to build a house for the Duke of Gordon's factor, William Mitchell. It survives today as Drumlin farmhouse.

In 1594, the castle played a minor part in history when Archibald Campbell, 7th Earl of Argyll, aka *Gillesbuig Grumach*, or Archibald the Grim (probably with a nod to his first wife's 14th century ancestor, Archibald Douglas, 3rd Earl of Douglas, who also rejoiced under that nickname), overnighted before the aforementioned Battle of Glenlivet.

The castle is now in the care of the Crown Estate and thanks to it having undertaken some stabilisation work, it can be visited by members of the public. The Crown Estate also owns Blairfindy Castle, which as you know, is also a work in progress.

We are leaving Glenlivet behind now and heading south-west down Strathavon on the B9136 where, in a short time, we come to the Tomintoul Distillery – since 1964, run and owned by Angus Dundee Distillers. Tours are available by appointment. It produces three million litres of single malt a year. In 2009, it featured in the *Guinness Book of Records* for producing the largest bottle of whisky in the world – 105.3 litres of a 14-year-old malt. That's more than 23 gallons. Even I couldn't get through that in a year, even with some help.

A little further on, we come to the "Soldier's Stone". You will need to be on the alert if you want to see it, as it is not easy to spot. It's on the right, a little pointy stone bearing the date 1690 with stone slabs on either side. It is said to be the grave of a fugitive from the Battle of Cromdale.

The precise date was 1st May 1690, and the battle took place on the other side of the Haughs of Cromdale in the shadow of *Creagan a'Chaise*, though a "rout" would be more semantically accurate. It is interesting to speculate the course history might have taken had the Jacobites' charismatic leader, "Bonnie Dundee", not fallen at Killiecrankie and then had gone on to follow up that victory with another at Dunkeld a month later on 21st August 1689 with Perth at his mercy. At Stirling, the Privy Council had already made plans to flee in that eventuality.

The commander at Dunkeld was Colonel Alexander Cannon, who was considered inept. Major-General Thomas Buchan was drafted in from Ireland to replace him. After the defeat at Dunkeld, the Highland army was dispirited, and over the winter of 1689-90 many melted away back home. From the 4,000 men who had been at Killiecrankie, it was a force of only 1,500 men that Buchan led into the Haughs of Cromdale, where he camped in sight of Grant Castle. This infuriated the laird, a government supporter and no lover of the Jacobites who were harrassing his lands. He sent word of the situation to Sir Thomas Livingstone, colonel in charge of the Royal Regiment of Scots dragoons at Inverness, who hastened south, arriving on the 28th April.

About three in the morning, on 1st May, with Grants as guides, while many of the Jacobites were still asleep, Livingstone made a surprise attack. In a letter to his boss, Major General Hugh Mackay, he claimed between three and

Tomintoul Distillery

The Soldier's Stone

Cromdale Hills

four hundred Jacobites were slain and a further hundred taken prisoner. The rest fled east over the Cromdale Hills. They were pursued, and many more would have fallen amongst the heather had not a mist come down and concealed them from their pursuers.

Whilst the accuracy of the figures may be questioned (you know how the victors write the history books), there is no doubt that this disaster effectively put a peep to the Jacobite cause in Scotland until the Rising of 1715. Nevertheless, the Jacobites somewhat cheekily claimed Cromdale as a victory, and a song, the *Haughs of Cromdale*, was written to celebrate the event. The last verse goes like this:

The loyal Stuarts, with Montrose,
So boldly set upon their foes,
And brought them down with Highland blows
Upon the Haughs of Cromdale.
Of twenty-thousand Cromwell's men,
Five hundred fled to Aberdeen,
The rest of them lie on the plain,
Upon the Haughs of Cromdale.

You will doubtless remember that Montrose, aka James Graham, 1st Marquess, had been executed in Edinburgh forty years previously, so if he *was* there, it must have been in spirit only. It's really quite astonishing, the Jacobite take on the event, the degree of propaganda. I suppose if you say it often enough and for long enough, people may start to believe it.

It is a lesson for our times.

Chapter Twenty

Grantown-on-Spey: The Very Model of a Modern Town and a Castle

THE B9136 joins the A939 just after the old Bridge of Avon, which was built by Caulfeild in 1754 as part of the Old Military Road. A plaque tells us it was earlier known as the "Bridge of Campaldore". The smaller of the two arches was destroyed on $2^{nd}/3^{rd}$ August 1829 in the *Muckle Spate*. It was repaired two years later. In 1990, a new bridge was built downstream to carry the A939 over the river, and at long last the old bridge was able to go into well deserved semi-retirement as a footbridge.

It's a good place to have a picnic, a very scenic spot. One person who thought so too was local historian and diplomat Sir Edward Peck (1915-2009) and his wife Lady Allison, who, as a cairn erected by the Crown Estate and Tomintoul Community Association in 2010 tells us, were great lovers of this area and who ensured the conservation of the bridge.

Not so lucky is another Caulfeild bridge built the same year, just a little to the north, and which is in a very serious state of disrepair. It's the very English-sounding Bridge of Brown, in Scots, *Brig o' Broon*, in Gaelic, *Drochaid Bhruthainn,* where the second word is pronounced "Vroon" meaning "bridge of boiling water". Thus this English name in the heart of the Highlands is explained.

Between the two bridges is a curious feature known as the "Fodderletter Lum". It's an ordinary-looking chimney such as might belong to a ruined cottage, only what is extraordinary about this *lum* is that it never formed part of

Road from Tomintoul to Grantown

Memorial at Old Bridge of Avon

any stone dwelling. What it *did* form part of was a wooden hut which workmen in charge of repairing the road erected in the 1920s, and where they could bed down for the night in relative warmth and comfort, and make something warm for their supper. It continued to be in use during the 1930s, and was restored by the Crown Estate and the Scottish Conservation Projects Trust in 1996.

One thing the Old Bridge of Brown has in common with the Old Bridge of Avon is it has been replaced with a new bridge which carries us effortlessly over the Burn of Brown towards Grantown. Just before the town, on the southern banks of the Spey, we meet the A95. Right leads to Cromdale and onwards to Aberlour. We turn left and, after a few yards, we arrive at Grantown East.

A former railway station originally belonging to the Speyside Line and later the Great North of Scotland Railway, Grantown East opened on 1st July 1863, although it was not yet known by that name. It took whisky south and brought day-trippers north from Aberdeen via Craigellachie and Boat of Garten.

Disaster struck in 1866 when the station was destroyed by fire. It was rebuilt but it was only a stay of execution, albeit a lengthy one. The last ever passengers alighted at 1.28pm precisely on 2nd November 1968, on what was called the "Speyside Excursion". "Excursion" makes it sound like a fun day out, whereas in actual fact it was bringing them to the station's funeral. Four minutes later, the train that brought them pulled out. Baron Beeching had pulled the plug on the line, just as he had done to so many others.

However, better times lay ahead. Exactly fifty years later, on 2nd November 2018, at 1.32pm precisely, Jim Telfer (95), the last signalman on the line, picked up his green flag once more and the Highland Heritage and Cultural Centre was declared open.

In the former station building, you can learn not only about the history of the railway, but that of the Highland Games, the making of the kilt, and – somewhat surprisingly – the Clydesdale horse. The centre has its very own tartan designed by Karen Blessington (owner of the Revack Estate), and Margaret Grant: purple for the heather, green for the trees, blue and white for the railway logo, plum for the windows of the station building, and black for the railway tracks.

In addition to that, you can act the giant as you sit astride a carriage on the 7.25 inch Revack miniature railway. It's a third of a mile long but plans are afoot to extend it by as much again. There is also a Highland Games field where it is planned to give demonstrations. That said, the main attraction of the centre is the restaurant – two refurbished railway carriages. Pizza is the speciality, savoury and sweet (!), baked in a Pompeii style wood-burning oven.

Grantown East Railway Centre

Oh, and I nearly forgot: there is also a shop where you can buy a souvenir!

Taking our leave, we cross the river and come to Grantown-on-Spey (as the town was renamed by the Town Council in 1898). The original settlement was at Cromdale, two miles to the east of the present town, but when the Old Military Road was built in 1754, the village found itself by-passed – perhaps the first instance of this ever happening in Scotland. Now the new town finds itself by-passed by the A95. *Plus ça change...*

You may find it hard to credit this, but Grantown was named after a man named Grant. The man in question was Sir James Grant (1738-1811), 8th Baronet. He succeeded his father as MP for Elginshire in 1761, and held the post until 1768. From 1790-95, he was MP for Banffshire. Under the guidance of his tutor, William Lorimer, he became a leading figure of the Scottish Enlightenment, interested in agricultural reform, but unlike other lairds who encouraged their tenants to emigrate, or even forcibly removed them from the land to make room for sheep, Sir James saw it as his duty to improve the lot of his tenants.

He was a man with a plan to build a new town. In April 1765, when he was a mere Mr – along with his father, Sir Ludovic Grant, who had handed over the bulk of the estate to him two years' previously – he placed advertisements in the press inviting people to come and settle. The first stone was laid in June 1765: a linen "manufactory" with a house. In October, the first settlers moved into their new houses which were built of stone with slate roofs. They must have seemed the height of luxury compared to the humble turf dwellings they were accustomed to. Not only that, they had big gardens at the rear in which they could grow their own food. What was not to like? (Two houses dating from 1768 are still standing in the Square. You will find them next to the Court House which was built a century later.)

Sir James also introduced wool-combing and stocking-making. Additionally, he brought water into the town. And when the harvests failed as a result of bad weather, he dipped into his own pocket to buy grain for his tenants and clansmen, thus earning him the soubriquet the "Good Sir James".

He was also very keen on the planting of trees for the timber industry. Wood was needed to build warships and make water pipes for other new towns being built. The logs were lashed together to make a raft which two intrepid oarsmen rode downriver to Speymouth, like Huckleberry Finn and Jim on the Mississippi. They were assisted by men on the bank equipped with long poles with iron hooks at the end called *cleeks*, with which they tried to manoeuvre obstacles out of the way.

Meanwhile, on dry land, an orphanage – aka the Speyside Charity School, thanks to the generosity of Lady Jane Grant of Monymusk – was founded in 1795. It was the very first orphanage in the Highlands. On hearing of the scheme, the Good Sir James gave it a home in the former Grammar School on the Square. Unfortunately, in 1817 the roof began to cave in. The solution was to reduce the width of the roof by moving the front wall of the building back from the street. This, however, upset Sir James's carefully laid-out street plan. The solution to *that* was to build a clock and bell tower with the money left over from that raised in 1813 by the patriotic townspeople to aid the "Russian Sufferers" during the Napoleonic Wars. The bell and clock were removed in 1975 and the former orphanage was converted into flats in the 1980s with the prestigious address of Speyside House.

The clock was finally restored in 2006 and has found a new home in the museum, whilst the bell is housed in a purpose-built campanile of wood shingles which stands outside the museum. It surely must be the most unusual bell tower in all of Scotland.

Another building of note is the Garth Hotel on Castle Road. It was built by Sir James's clerk and the oldest part, dating from 1769, still remains. In its long life, it has gone through several transformations including being the summer home of the exotic-sounding Victorian novelist Marie Corelli (1855-1924), whose real name was Mary Mackay. Her father was man-of-letters, Dr Charles Mackay; her mother was Elizabeth Mills, a servant in the household and whom he later married. In her day, believe it or not, Ms Corelli outsold Conan Doyle, H.G. Wells and Kipling *combined.* See what the right name can do for sales! Would the same number of punters have bought books by Mary Mackay, one wonders? It is fair to point out she is not read much nowadays. Still, it was good while it lasted.

Bell Tower at Grantown Museum

One of the first residents was Mrs McKenzie who was given the feu, or long lease, of an inn. In the event, the lease lasted longer than she did in the town. After falling out with some residents, she took herself and her business to Tomintoul – where, you may recall, I introduced her to you earlier.

By 1801, the population of Sir James's pet project had risen to 435, with 42 employed in the woollen industry. Other trades were attracted to the town: butchers, bakers and candle-makers, as well as smiths, carpenters, shoemakers, and so on. The usual suspects. Seventy years after Sir James went to heaven (as he most surely must have), a hospital was built in 1881.

As well as being a town-founder, the Good Laird was also a supporter of the arts. In 1770, he sent John Cumming, a son of his piper, to the McArthur College of Piping at Kilmuir in Skye. His father, Angus, was one of the town's earliest settlers, and his collection of *Strathspey or Old Highland Reels* was published posthumously in 1780.

Grant's greatest contribution to the arts, however, was when, in 1783, he was one of the two co-founders of the Royal Society of Scotland. Incidentally, in another tenuous contribution to the arts, his sister, Penuel, was married to Henry McKenzie (1745-1831), the so-called "Addison of the North". (You see why I mentioned this.)

Sir James died at the family seat of Grant Castle, where he was born. He was succeeded by his son, Lewis Alexander Grant, who later that year succeeded his second cousin as 5th Earl of Seafield. Sadly, Lewis suffered from mental illness and never married. He was succeeded by his younger brother, Francis William Ogilvy-Grant, who had already taken over the management of the estates.

The history of the castle goes back as far as 1536, when a Z-shaped tower house was built on the lands which had been in the ownership of Sir Duncan le Gaunte of Fruychy since the middle of the 15th century. It was known as *Ballachastell*, that is to say "the town of the castle", and also as "Castle Freuchy". It was given its present name of Castle Grant by Ludovic Grant in 1694, and remained in the hands of the Grants for nearly five centuries. During WWII it served as a barracks. Unfortunately, the army gave it too much tender loving care. Wet rot and damp set in as a result of too much mopping of the floors and the castle became uninhabitable.

At the end of the 17th century, the Grants supported the Covenanters and, during the Jacobite risings, they were on the Government side. They paid the price for that in 1715 when the castle was occupied by the Jacobites. In the '45, the Laird remained neutral. Fat lot of good it did him. The Jacobites occupied the castle again anyway.

Between 1753 and 1783, John Adam from the celebrated family of architects, made alterations to the castle including the construction of a mansion across the north face of the building and which now became the main entrance. Burns spent "half a day with Sir James and family" in 1787, and Queen Victoria and Prince Albert visited the policies in 1860. She was not impressed, describing them as having "a fine (not Highland-looking) park with a very plain-looking house, like a factory".

The castle was restored by Sir Robert Lorimer in 1912, but it later became derelict. It is a fine thing to have a big *hoose*, but it's another thing entirely to be able to maintain it.

In the 1990s it was restored again and bought for £720,000 by Craig Whyte, who famously led Rangers F.C. into administration and liquidation in 2012. The Bank of Scotland repossessed it after he failed to keep up the £7,000-a-month mortgage payments, but not before he had allegedly spent £5m on restorations and renovations.

It was bought for a cool £1 million in September 2014 by the ex-CEO of the Russian Author Society, Sergey Fedotov, who defrauded the society of £4m of the authors' royalty payments. He too spent thousands of pounds of their money in refurbishing the castle from top to toe. He was arrested in Moscow in 2016, and the castle was put up for sale. It comes with 35 acres of grounds and has a drawing room, ballroom, billiard room, library and cinema room, to name just a few. Part of the second floor consists of a 2-bedroomed self-contained flat.

In addition to that, like all self-respecting castles, it has a ghost, which comes at no added cost. The spectre is supposedly Lady Barbara Grant, who died of a broken heart in the 16th century when her father refused to let her marry the man she loved because he thought he was below her station. He picked someone else whom he saw as more fitting but she refused to comply. As a punishment, he shut her up in a closet in the tower until she came to her senses – a sort of medieval form of the naughty step. It was hidden behind tapestries and called "The Blackness". The lady, however, was not for changing her mind. She would rather die first – and she did.

She has been seen materialising from behind the tapestry and wandering about the tower, wringing her hands like Lady Macbeth. The closet was opened by some brave men in the 1880s, and guess what they found? Only some rusty old swords and muskets.

However, in our times, when the castle was being refurbished, workmen in a room near the tower heard footsteps there, a door opening and closing, voices, and the sound of someone crying. They didn't actually *see* anything, but they were sufficiently spooked to refuse to work there at night ever again...

Chapter Twenty-One

Grantown-on-Spey: Trains and Toilets

QUEEN Victoria once overnighted at the Grant Arms – allegedly the first time she had stayed in public premises – but not the one we see today, which dates from 1875. Before its predecessor became a hotel, it was a brewery – an attempt by the Good Sir James to wean the villagers off the strong stuff being concocted in the plethora of illicit stills in the area. It didn't last long, however, after its inception in 1780.

In another development which Sir James didn't live to see – which is maybe just as well, given his views on the strong stuff – in 1824, James McGregor was granted a licence to turn his illicit still in Cromdale into the Balmenach Distillery. It continued to be operated by the family until 1922. It closed down in 1993 but, after being bought by Inver House Distillers, it began production again in 1998. It produces one of the five single malts which goes into the making of the wonderfully-named Hankey Bannister blend – a favourite of Sir Winston Churchill.

In 2009, the distillery also began producing Caorunn gin in 1,000 litre batches. The bottle helpfully tells you it is pronounced "ka-roon", the Gaelic for "rowan berry". It is one of the 11 botanicals which goes into creating its unique taste, including five hand-foraged ones. It is no secret that some of the others include heather, bog myrtle and – wait for it – dandelion leaves.

A year after the Queen's visit, the population of Grantown had risen to 1,334. Wow! That's twice as big as it is today! In fact, her visit gave a

The Grant Arms Hotel

The Square at Grantown

much-needed boost to the economy, since if it was good enough for her, her citizens reckoned it must be good enough for them. And it was just as well as, by this time, the linen industry – up till then the main employer of the town – had collapsed as a result of cheaper imports from the Baltic.

This influx of tourists was facilitated with the arrival of the Inverness and Perth Junction Railway, with the 36-mile section between Forres and Aviemore being opened on 1st June 1863. That said, the owners of the railway had four-legged passengers and fish in mind rather than people, the aim being to transport them to markets in the south. Incredibly, what took four or six weeks by road was reduced to a single day by rail! In 1867, the line transported 21,000 sheep – no, not in a year, but in one *week*!

The route to Forres, over moor and mountain, was at the mercy of the weather. The winter of 1880/81 was particularly cruel. On 17th December, a train had to be abandoned just south of Dava station during a snowstorm. The passengers managed to make it to the station whilst the storm raged. After it was all over, they found the train buried under 60 feet of snow. Meanwhile, at the other end of the station, another train carrying passengers and cattle was similarly stuck in drifts. The people made it to safety, but the cattle died of suffocation. A relief train also became stuck. It was a winter that wouldn't easily be forgotten.

By this time, Sir James's grandson, John Charles Ogilvy-Grant, aka the 7th Earl of Seafield, had succeeded to the estate as well as that of Seafield. Normally landowners jealously guarded their privacy and were no fans of the huffing, puffing steam monsters and diverted the railway lines away from their castles or mansions, often resulting in a serious detour between towns. Here, however, the 7th Earl allowed the Inverness and Perth Junction Railway line to pass through the north-west of his estate. "In acknowledgement of the great facilities given by the Earl in the formation of the railway through his estates," as the company put it, it built him his own private station where the train would halt by demand to pick him and his entourage up. Some station, some waiting room! A lodge by any other name, it was recently put on the market for £335,000.

As you already know, on 1st July of that same year, a rival line was built by what later became the Great North of Scotland Railway whose station was at Grantown East. For such a small population, the town certainly was well-served by rail. And the people flocked here because of its growing reputation as a healthy sort of place. As one report in the 1890s put it: "In no other part of Scotland are there more octogenarians and nonagenarians to be found." (Keep your eyes open. See how may you can spot as you walk around.)

And so, at last, in this narrative, we come to the museum – though actually it is where we began our exploration of the town. It started out as a Victorian girls' school and still is in the education business, informing locals and visitors alike about the life and times of the town. And very well-presented it is too, beginning with a short video.

One of the main exhibits is the Cromdale brooch which is thought to date from the 17th century. It is displayed in a case showing how it would have been worn to pin the edges of women's shawls or *arisaids* together. A functional part of Highland dress certainly, but the artistic detail engraved on this brooch is quite extraordinary. It features wild cats and is thought, therefore, to have once belonged to a member of Clan Chattan. As anyone who has even had a rudimentary exposure to French knows, *chat* means "cat", hence the design on the brooch.

Clan Chattan was a confederation of smaller clans who united to form an alliance against their more powerful neighbours and enemies, such as the Grants. Its motto, along with the Macphersons, and several others in the Confederation, is *Touch not the cat bot a glove*. As anyone in possession of a domestic pussycat knows, before attempting to stuff the feline quadruped into a carrier for a visit to the vet, one should always don a stout pair of gardening gloves ahead of attempting the manoeuvre. For a greater challenge, try doing that with a wild cat, if first you can catch one as Mrs Glasse's *Art of Cookery* (1747) didn't quite say, with reference to a hare.

Courtesy of the museum, may I offer you this bit of trivia? Who, do you think, invented the flushing toilet? And for a bonus point, what has that to do with Grantown?

Well, the Romans had a flushing system long, long ago, as did other civilisations, but if we are talking about the sort of thing that we have in our homes today, then the honour must go to Sir John Harrington, godson of Elizabeth I and a courtier, who invented such a device as early as 1596. The snag was it required 7.5 gallons of water, which was stored in an overhead cistern. In the days before interior plumbing, this was a bit of a chore to top up to say the least, especially when tummy upsets occurred – which I imagine they did quite frequently. Fortunately, those in the possession of the new invention were also in possession of a goodly number of servants.

If we are talking about the first practical flush toilet, which we are, then the honour goes to Alexander Cumming (1773-1814), whose bright idea was the S-bend which trapped water in the bowl and eliminated nasty smells coming from where the solids had just been dispatched. Although born in Edinburgh, his parents came from Duthil near here, and incidentally, the burial place of the Grants.

His invention was improved by the unfortunately (or appropriately) named Thomas Crapper who converted the S-bend below the bowl to a U-bend and who also invented the floating ballcock. Most people erroneously think *he* was the inventor of the flush toilet, because he manufactured vast quantities of them bearing his name. In its abbreviated form, the name has come into common parlance for the bodily function, but in actual fact the word was coined in medieval times.

He was undoubtedly a great man but I can't help but think that when it came to the matter of finding a wife, being in possession of a surname like that would have presented something of a deterrent for prospective brides. Well, how would you like to be known as Mrs Crapper? However, I am happy to tell you that is exactly what happened to Miss Maria Green.

But back to Alexander Cumming, who was the real inventor of the first flush toilet. That was just one of his accomplishments. He was also a clockmaker, mathematician, mechanic and instrument maker. He made a barometric clock for George III in 1765 and was paid £15 a year to maintain it. Nice work if you can invent it. In 1783, he was one of the joint founders of the Royal Society of Edinburgh for the advancement of learning and knowledge, who made him a Fellow. (And I should think so too.) He also has the distinction of having an island named after him – Cummingøya in the Svalbard archipelago – after he made instruments for Captain Phipp's voyage of exploration to the North Pole in 1773.

Two more people of note with a Grantown connection are Peter Grant of the Songs, aka *Pàdraig Grannd nan Oran* (1783-1867), who was Grantown's Baptist pastor for 41 years. His *Dain Spioadail,* a

The Old Spey Bridge

The Charles Hay Memorial

book of spiritual songs in the Gaelic, was published when he was only twenty-six. It was popular all over the Highlands, as well as in the American colonies. His son succeeded him at the same church, where he ministered to his flock for 39 years. Talk about cornering the market! Finally, James Kerr (1863-1928), opened a pharmacy in Grantown in 1887 and was one of the first people to make use of Wilhelm Röntgen's discovery of X-rays in 1895.

Thank you, Grantown Museum – that was very informative. Now we're back on the trail of the more distant past. The appropriately-named Forest Road morphs into the Old Military Road and heads east along the riverbank. And there, on a narrow bend of the river, it meets the Old Spey Bridge, built in 1754.

Walking across it, we find a stone marker, similar to the one at the Well of Lecht. It is better preserved, though like it, part of the left-hand side is missing. Similarly, it also utilises the same economy of space by combining letters. It reads thus:

D·
E· COMPANEIS·
OF · THE · 33D · REG
EMENT · THE · RIGHT ·
HONOURABLE · LORD
CHARLES · HAY ·
COLONEL

ENDED

It resonates, it really does, down all these years, that last word – you can practically feel the relief with which the anonymous sculptor laid down, not so much his chisel, but his road-making tools. You get the feeling he would have liked to have carved an exclamation mark, if only he had had any energy left to do so.

Chapter Twenty-Two

Huntly's Cave and Duthil: A Hidey-Hole and a Cemetery

THE Iron Horse may have gone long ago but it has left a legacy in that the disused tracks on the Inverness and Perth Junction Railway provide a handy path for Shanks's pony, now reborn as the "Dava Way". It opened in 2005 and connects with the Moray Coast Trail and the Speyside Way. All three feature on Scottish Natural Heritage (SNH) list of Scotland's Great Trails.

The Speyside Way runs from Buckie, initially along the coast to Spey Bay, before heading inland and over the hills far away to Aviemore, 66 miles down the Spey valley. There is also a spur from Ballindalloch to Tomintoul, a distance of fifteen miles and which rises to 1,800 feet, not just once but twice. It is labelled as "challenging". It will take you about 35 hours' walking time, including the spur, but there are plenty of places to stay overnight and of course you can start at the other end if you prefer. And you can bike it most of the way rather than hike, if that suits you better.

At 45 miles long, the Moray Coastal Trail does in no way contravene the Trades' Description Act, since it follows the coast from Forres to Cullen. The SNH recommends walking it from west to east on account of the prevailing winds. Ignore that advice at your peril.

At 24 miles long, the Dava Way is the shortest of the three and, if that is too short for those boots that were made for walking, you can connect with the other two and do the circular 95-mile-long Moray Way.

Three miles to the north of the town, on the Dava Way, a little detour takes walkers and climbers to Huntly's Cave which lies in a ravine cut by the *Alt an Fhithich* (Burn of the Raven). It is named after George Gordon, 2nd Marquis of Huntly, whom we met in Chapter Twelve. It is said to be one of the places where he hid when he was on the run after being defeated by Archibald Campbell, 1st Marquess of Argyll (1598-1661). You may remember he was held at Blairfindy before being executed in Edinburgh in 1649.

What's good enough for the father is good enough for the son. Lewis Gordon, 3rd Marquess of Gordon (1626-53), also hid here after there was a falling-out over tactics. The Gordons wanted to harry the north, whereas Montrose wanted to march south. Anyway, whilst he was hiding in the cave, Gordon was looked after by Mary Grant, a sister of the Good Sir James. The story has a happy ending as he married her and they had three daughters and a son. Not only that, but he converted her to Catholicism. Alas the marriage was not destined to last long. He died aged only 27. The Lord giveth and the Lord taketh away.

Mind you, he packed a lot of living into that short time. When he was still a child, he stole some jewels and tried to take ship to Holland – a hotbed of Protestantism at the time – with the intention of joining the army. For a child of his religious persuasion, it would have been like jumping into a fire.

Back home, he didn't improve his precocious behaviour any. When he was thirteen, he sneaked out of Gordon Castle to rally his father's men against the Covenanters, led at that time by Montrose. The armies met at Melgray Hill and, when the Gordons came under cannon fire, discretion became the better part of valour and they retired to Aberdeen instead of staying to put up a fight.

After that humiliation, Lewis went to France for three years to learn his craft – how to win battles – before returning to England where he fought for the Royalists in the English Civil War. Then in an amazing volte-face, he fought for the Covenanters under his uncle, Alistair Campbell, 8th Earl of Argyll (1607-61).

He was only sixteen when he returned home. In a story of brotherly love which brings Cain and Abel to mind, and which John Steinbeck reprised in *East of Eden,* while his older brother was in England, having fled there in fear of his life, he seduced his fiancée, the Mary Grant aforesaid.

Sometimes history can be complicated and confusing, especially so when the main protagonists change sides. You may remember that James Graham, 1st Marquess of Montrose, initially was a Covenanter but later fought for Charles I. It is interesting to reflect that Montrose was convinced God was on his side when he fought as a Covenanter – so when he switched sides, did God also?

There is an earlier legend from the 14th century which pertains to Huntly's hidey-hole. The story goes that a son of Grant of Stratherrick, on the south-east shore off Loch Ness, ran off with the daughter of a MacGregor chieftain and took refuge in the cave. It was Comyn territory in those days, and the Chief was far from amused by the new lodgers setting up home without as much as a by-your-leave – for the couple did not come alone, but brought a retinue of men, which apart from not being very romantic, I would say was bit silly in those times of inter-clan rivalry and warfare. To show his displeasure, the Comyn began harassing the interlopers.

Eventually the MacGregor Chief and his men caught up with the lovers and, instead of reading the riot act to his would-be son-in-law as you would expect, the wrath of the MacGregors was appeased when they were welcomed very warmly – even given a feast as if the runaways were living with all the comforts a castle could provide instead of a draughty old cave. All was forgiven and, what's more, the MacGregors agreed to form an alliance against the Comyns.

They didn't waste any time. The very next day, they stormed the Comyns' stronghold. The Comyn was killed in the fray, and Grant cut off his head and kept it as a trophy. In what is the best use of a skull I have heard of since Byron used one as a wine glass, the top was sawn off, fitted with a hinge and converted into a very handy container for odds and ends. It is said if the skull ever leaves the possession of the Grants, they will lose all their lands in Strathspey. You would have thought they would have guarded this heirloom zealously, but – strange to relate – where it is now, no-one knows.

The outstanding rock (in more ways than one), above the cave, is very popular with climbers. Geologists amongst you might like to know that is formed of foliated blocks of schist which were uplifted during the Caledonian Orogeny, uplifted from the Iapetus Ocean about 470 million years ago. Don't say I didn't tell you.

There is another treat in store for those who get off on rocks not far to the south, just off the A95 at Dulnain Bridge – the *roches moutonnées* (literally "fleecy rocks") – and that is where we are heading now. The term was coined in 1787 by the Swiss geologist, H.B. Saussure (1740-99), aka the Founder of Alpinism. He was also a meteorologist, physicist, and inventor of the solar oven. He thought those kind of rocks resembled the curly wigs worn by barristers today and by men of yesteryear. In those days they were slicked down with mutton tallow, the Brylcreem of its day, only not so sweet-smelling. If you have ever seen a lamb's fleece close

The *Roches Moutonnées*

up, you can see why M. Saussure must have been so sure it was an apt comparison.

A handy pair of notices on a specially-shaped cairn explains what is unusual about these rocks. We are told that about 18,000 years ago this land was covered by an ice sheet more than two thousand feet thick. Imagine that! Half as high as Ben Nevis! As the ice moved, it left striations on the rocks beneath. They occur as outcrops, usually in groups, just as the glacier dumped them before it retreated. These rocks are usually ovoid in shape, and you can tell the direction of the travel of the ice with one side gently-sloping where the ice had been, while the other is rough and steep, like a cliff.

Information Notice at *Roches Moutonnées*

We carry onward and westward towards Carrbridge on the A938, where the next point of interest is Duthil cemetery (probably named after St Dubhthac) – the burial ground of the Grants and the Earls of Seafield, as well as a goodly number of folks of the more common sort where moss-covered headstones mark their final resting place and where, unlike the Grants who are sound asleep tucked up in their mausoleum, they are condemned to anonymity as they are impossible to read.

The first Grant to be buried in the kirkyard was James "the Bold" Grant, 3rd Laird of Freuchy, in 1553. He was followed in death by his son, John "the Gentle" Grant in 1585. It tickles me, having a nickname as a sort of middle name that sums up your personality. I suppose it's one bestowed upon you by your friends or enemies. I wonder what mine would be. On reflection, it's probably better not to speculate too much.

There are so many dead Grants of note here, they had to build not just one, but *two* mausoleums. With their crenellated battlements and studded doors, they have much of a fortress sort-of-look about them. The first was built in 1837 and the second was sealed up in 1913 after receiving the body of the Dowager Countess in 1911 who expressed in her will that she did not wish to sleep the Big Sleep with any more than those already there, amongst others, the 5th, 6th, 7th and 8th Earls of Seafield, all Ogilvy-Grants – apart from the 5th Earl, who was the last Grant-Ogilvy. I don't know the reason for reversing the name order, but it does seem to me Ogilvy-Grant does have a better ring to it.

As far as the Old Parish Church is concerned, the first was built about 1400 and dedicated to St Peter, probably on the site of an earlier church. In its turn, over the years, it spawned several others. The last one was in 1826 and it closed in 1967. However, it was born again as the Clan Grant Centre and Museum, open by appointment.

Duthil Cemetery

The first Protestant minister, William Fraser, was only inducted in 1614 – 54 years after the Reformation. Isn't that a remarkable thing! Fast forward two centuries to 1843 when, after the Disruption, the faithful of Duthil worshipped in the woods in all weathers for three hours every Sunday until the Free Church was built in 1850. That's dedication. They don't make them as hardy as that any more.

A noticeboard at the entrance to the cemetery informs us that Gregor Grant, Sheriff of Inverness (c.1200) was the first "prominent" Grant and that his line can be traced to the present 33rd Chief, Sir James Grant of Grant, 6th Lord Strathspey. Not a lot of people can trace their ancestry as far back as that, let alone having it all handed to them on a plate.

During the Wars of Independence, the Grants supported Wallace and Bruce. Being a supporter of the latter was a smart move as he confirmed them as lords and masters of Strathspey. In the 18th century, however, the majority of the clan were Government supporters, though as in the best well-regulated families, some supported the other side – just as, in our times, Brexit divided friends as well as families.

Grant Mausoleums, Duthil

The clan motto is "Standfast Craig Ellachie" named after the mountain which dominates Aviemore, aka the the "Rock of Alarm" on top of which a beacon was lit to warn the clan of danger, or call men to arms. This is echoed in the clan crest which shows the top of a mountain on fire. And while on the subject, I may as well mention that the clan symbol is the Scots pine.

Turning to the ministers of Duthil, one of the most memorable was the Rev. James Bain (1828-1911), the incumbent from 1877 until his death in 1911, and no friend of the Seafield Estates. In 1885, he took Caroline, the Countess Dowager of Seafield, to the Court of Session – the highest court in all the land – complaining that the manse was insanitary due to its proximity to the kirkyard, which he said was too full and too shallow. He also claimed the mausoleums were a danger to his health because the coffins were stored above ground. He won his case with regard to the manse but not the mausoleums. Like a latter-day John Knox, who famously published the pamphlet *A Trumpet Blast Against The Monstrous Regiment of Women*, Bain published his own: *The Seafield Mausoleums and Duthil Churchyard Case. A specimen of how officials tamper with the law in Scotland when they want to serve the great.*

The Countess must have regarded him as a real thorn in her side, but she wasn't his only target, just the nearest. He was generally opposed to what he saw as a culture of deference to landlords in the Highlands, saw himself as a champion of the poor – of the "masses against the classes", echoing a quote from William Ewart Gladstone in a speech he made in 1886.

Although he died in Duthil, you will search in vain for Bain's grave there. He was taken back to his roots in Dingwall and that is where you will find him, pushing up the daisies in St Clement's Churchyard.

Chapter Twenty-Three

Carrbridge and Boat of Garten: A Bridge and a Bird

WE continue on our way to Carrbridge, where the 30mph sign tells us this is the home of the Golden Spurtle World Porridge-Making Championship. It has been held annually since October 1994 and draws competitors from all over the world. Strange but true. The sign also features a drawing of a packhorse bridge and tells us that the town's Gaelic name is *Drochaid Chàrr*, which means the "bridge at the marsh".

The said bridge crosses the river Dulnain, and during the *Muckle Spate* of 1829, its parapets were swept away so all that remains now is a fragile-looking slender arch which stretches incredibly high and gracefully over the river. It was commissioned by Brigadier-General Sir Alexander Grant, Clan Chief, and built by John Niccelsone, a mason from Ballindalloch, in 1717 at the cost of £100. It is the oldest remaining bridge in the Highlands, well worth coming to see for that reason alone, never mind it being so photogenic. It is also known as the "Coffin Bridge" because mourners used it to carry their loved ones over it to the cemetery at Duthil, which, in my view, makes it even more interesting.

Wade's two-arch Sluggan Bridge was built a few years later three miles to the west. Enter road builder *extraordinaire* Thomas Telford who, when he re-mapped the roads to the north, eschewed Wade's bridge in favour of Niccelsone's. It also fell victim to the *Muckle Spate*, only it fared even worse: it was completely swept away. It was later replaced by a single-arch bridge.

The Old Bridge, Carrbridge

In the fullness of time, Telford's route became the A9 and ran through Carrbridge until the 1970s, when it took a jink a little to the west and bypassed the town. The railroad was extended from Aviemore in 1894 and, three years later, it went all the way to Inverness. It is one of the rare survivors of Beeching's cuts: the station and the line still exist.

Carving at Carrbridge

Carrbridge also plays host to Carve Carrbridge, a Chainsaw Carving Competition, held annually in September and which has been running since 2002. Like the porridge-making, it also attracts competitors from all over the world. Once the competition is over, the sculptures are sold off by auction. You can see some examples of past competitions dotted about the town.

Manipulating a heavy and unwieldy chain-saw to carve out delicate shapes and figures from a log, I would have thought, requires a whole set of different skills from the elbow-bending required to stir a *spurtle* in a pot of what Dr Johnson insultingly referred to "what in England feeds the horses but which in Scotland feeds the people". It's hard to see how anyone could make a competition out of making porridge but Carrbridge does, and the decision of whoever is declared the winner is not so much in the hands of the judges, but on their tastebuds.

Another attraction Carrbridge has to offer is the Landmark Forest Adventure Park – a great day out for the kids with a Dinosaur Kingdom, Butterfly House, Runaway Timber Train, Lost Labyrinth, Wild Water Coaster and much, much more. You get the idea.

Boat of Garten Railway Station

Not having any kids with us, we take the B9153 out of town and then the A95 towards Boat of Garten. It bypasses the village, however on 3rd August 1863, the Inverness and Perth Junction Railway (later the Highland Railway) drove straight into its heart, connecting it with Aviemore and Forres over the Dava Summit. It was also a junction for the Speyside branch to Craigellachie on the Great North of Scotland Railway.

You will find the station, which took its name from the ferry that used to operate here, behind the present-day Boat Hotel. The railway's principal use was to transport the local products of whisky, livestock and timber to the south. Before that, as I mentioned earlier, the logs were floated down the river, but – as all malt whisky aficionados know – water and whisky should only come together in moderation.

Like so many others, the line fell victim to the Beeching cuts. Passenger services were chopped on 18th October 1965 and freight followed on 16th June 1968. As things turned out, it was only a short time before passenger services resumed again. A group of volunteers formed the Strathspey Railway Association in 1971 and on 22nd July 1978 – just ten years after the last train departed – the first train puffed out of Boat of Garten bound for Aviemore, the southern terminus. Aviemore also serves as a maintenance centre and is where locomotives are sheltered in sheds overnight. The whole operation is entirely run by hard-working volunteers who do everything from running, restoring, and maintaining the trains, to making the teas in the dining carriage.

The present station buildings, which include two platforms, two signal boxes and a water tower, date from 1904 and were designed by William Roberts. On 15th July 2019, one of the workshops was badly damaged by fire.

The station is a minor film star. It featured in the very first episode of ITV's *Dr Finlay's Casebook*, starring David Rintoul in the title role with Ian Bannen as Dr Cameron and Annette Crosbie as Janet. It is set in the 1940s as Dr Finlay returns from the War, and the storylines have much to do with the setting up of the nascent NHS. It was first broadcast on 3rd March 1993 and ran for four series until 20th December 1996.

The northern terminus of the railway is at Broomhill. The station there was entirely rebuilt on the footprint of the old one during the 1990s and opened in 2002. Fans of *Monarch of the Glen*, based on the books by Sir Compton Mackenzie (1883-1972), and which ran from 2000-05 on BBC1, might recognise it as Glenbogle Station, and for those who never watched it (like me), a board proudly tells

Loch Garten

them so.

Plans are afoot to extend the ten miles of track to Grantown. In 2014, a major obstacle was overcome when a bridge was built over the River Dulnain. Other obstacles to completing the dream remain – not least, of course, finding the wherewithall.

RSBP Osprey Centre, Loch Garten

Boat of Garten is alternatively known as the "Osprey Town" and the RSPB centre, which is open from April to August, is only a mile to the east on the wooded shores of Loch Garten. In 1916, ospreys became extinct in Scotland, but then a breeding pair from Scandinavia built a nest in 1954. Five years later, they were the only breeding pair in the UK. The nest had to be protected around the clock from egg collectors. Their efforts were well rewarded. The birds bred successfully and, in due course – as all parents hope, and as all children should – they flew the nest. There are now about 250 pairs nesting in Britain.

The most recent and prolific female was EJ, who successfully reared 23 chicks from 2003. Her life was not without tragedy, however. In 2017, her long-term mate, Odin, died. It is thought he was killed by a rival for EJ's hand, so to speak. Sadly he was not the only casualty – their three chicks starved to death because it was his job to bring back, not so much the bacon, but the fish, while she stayed at home and looked after the kids.

I'm sorry to to have to say that the bad news does not stop there. In the spring of 2019, EJ did not return. Did she balk, at her age, at the thought of the 3,000-mile flight from Africa? I wouldn't blame her. Nowadays I find long-haul flights tedious enough, and I have nothing more strenuous to do than sit on my *bahookey*. Of course that's only speculation – she may have been involved in an air disaster en route or died of natural causes. The possibilities are many, and it's unlikely we shall ever know what happened to her. Whatever it was, sadly, it looks like the end of an era.

The empty nest is in the Abernethy Forest, part of which is a remnant of the ancient Caledonian Forest that once covered a huge area of Scotland but of which only 1% remains today. The trees are mainly Scots pine, but there are also juniper, rowan, and birch, while on the forest floor, there are blaeberry and heather. It is home to some of Scotland's rarest birds and mammals such as the Scottish crossbill, the capercaillie, pine martens and the elusive wildcat. There are more common residents besides, such as black grouse, crested tits, red squirrels and deer.

I am getting very near to the end of this narrative now, but before we head back to Grantown and from whence we came, I want to tell you a story, as Max Bygraves famously began his routine.

Once upon a time, just a little to the north of the village, near the motte-and-bailey castle of Tom Pitlac, there used to be a stone which was erected to the memory of a lady who dwelt in medieval times. She knew she was not much longer for this world and her dying wish was to be buried with her husband, Peter Grant. Unfortunately, there was a problem. He lay on the other side of the Spey, which happened to be in spate. The lady was not for turning back. "Go you to the water-side where I tell you and a passage will be speedily effected." You've got to hand it to the lady – she had a fine turn of phrase for someone whose last breath was imminent.

And *lo!* it turned out just as she said, for when she did indeed take her last breath and when the funeral cortège arrived at the spot, the waters parted like the Red Sea did for the Children of Israel and they walked across dry-shod. On their way, they encountered a shoal of salmon who were surprised to find themselves suddenly out of their element. For the mourners, it was even easier than shooting fish in a barrel, and they were severely tempted to put down their burden and make the most of this unforeseen harvest. But the Spey is a wise old river and managed to return its denizens to its life-giving waters before the mourners could take advantage. And so the lady was taken safely to the other side and was laid to rest with her husband.

Skip forward a few centuries to 1865 and when the so-called five-foot high "Miracle Stone" was erected to commemorate the event. The prime mover behind this memorial was 92 year-old William Grant of Slochd (from the Gaelic *An Sloc*, meaning "the pit") near Carrbridge. (By the way, Slochd Summit is the highest pass on the A9 and the railway, 1328 and 1315 feet respectively.)

It came to William in a dream, as he lay on his deathbed, that a stone should be erected, inscribed in Gaelic and English, to mark the "signal manifestation of the Divine Power in dividing this water" – which just goes to show you that the lady was not the only one capable of spouting a fine turn of phrase on her deathbed. (God grant me the power to be so coherent on mine, and someone with a notebook and pencil to write them down for posterity.)

Actually, I have a serious point to make, which is that Mr Grant, aforesaid, was not just an ordinary geezer. He was a so-called "holy man", one of "The Men" – the Gaelic-speaking Calvinist "saints", easily recognisable with their long blue cloak, long hair and spotted hankie which they wore on their

Broomhill Station

head. They claimed to get results from their prayers, unlike the Free Kirk ministers, for whom they had little respect, despite all their book-learning.

The plot thickens. It turns out that the lady in the Dividing of the Waters story was not a medieval lady after all, but one who lived in the 17th century. She was known to the locals as "Holy Mary of Luirg", and considered by them to be rather saintly – a female equivalent of "The Men". The stone invoked the ire of the Free Kirk ministers enormously. They saw it as nothing less than "The Men" putting two fingers up to them, mocking them for not being able to perform wonders and miracles like they could. The ministers condemned the erection of the stone in the press, preached against it in the pulpits and then, losing patience, on 19th February 1867, a demolition squad was sent out to smash it to pieces and throw it in the river. A century later, local historian George Dixon braved the chilly waters and found the stone, mostly intact. And there it lies to this day.

So, leaving Boat of Garten and its stories behind, we head back to the A95, towards Grantown, calling in at Broomhill on the way. And that is how our Snow Roads Scenic Route came to an end, as all good things must. It's time to head for home, back the way we came.

Better informed now about the history of this ancient landscape, we shall see it in a more informed light, and as we head towards the hills, we shall them from a different perspective too. Maybe they'll look even better.

It's an exciting prospect.

Image Credits

The illustrations in this book are sourced from the personal photographic collection of the author, with the exception of the following images which are detailed below:

Page 17:	Image of Area Surrounding Ardblair Castle is Copyright © Mike Pennington and is licensed under the Creative Commons Attribution-Share Alike 2.0 Generic license (https://creativecommons.org/licenses/by-sa/2.0/deed.en). Wikimedia Commons.
Page 19:	Image of Rae Loch is Copyright © Alan Reid and is licensed under the Creative Commons Attribution-Share Alike 2.0 Generic license (https://creativecommons.org/licenses/by-sa/2.0/deed.en). Wikimedia Commons.
Page 19:	Image of Loch of Drumellie is Copyright © Mike Pennington and is licensed under the Creative Commons Attribution-Share Alike 2.0 Generic license (https://creativecommons.org/licenses/by-sa/2.0/deed.en). Wikimedia Commons.
Page 34:	Photo of Meigle Sculpted Stone Museum and the Daniel Stone taken by the author on the premises and reproduced by kind permission of Historic Environment Scotland.
Pages 74-76:	Photos of the interior of Braemar Castle taken by the author on the premises by kind permission of Braemar Castle.
Page 90:	Image of Abergeldie Castle is Copyright © Peter Gordon and is licensed under the Creative Commons Attribution-Share Alike 2.0 Generic license (https://creativecommons.org/licenses/by-sa/2.0/deed.en). Wikimedia Commons.
Page 91:	Image of Birkhall is Copyright © Alan Findlay and is licensed under the Creative Commons Attribution-Share Alike 2.0 Generic license (https://creativecommons.org/licenses/by-sa/2.0/deed.en). Wikimedia Commons.
Pages 94-95:	Photos of the interior of Ballater Visitor Centre taken by the author on the premises by kind permission of Ballater Visitor Centre.

About the Author

A native of Banff, Scotland, David M. Addison is a graduate of Aberdeen University. In addition to essays in various publications, he has written several books, mainly about his travels.

As well as a short spell teaching English as a foreign language in Poland when the Solidarity movement at its height, he spent a year (1978-79) as an exchange teacher in Montana.

He regards his decision to apply for the exchange as one of the best things he ever did, for not only did it give him the chance to travel extensively in the US and Canada but during the course of the year he made a number of enduring friendships.

Since taking early retirement (he is not as old as he looks), he has more time but less money to indulge his unquenchable thirst for travel (and his wife would say for Cabernet Sauvignon and malt whisky). He is doing his best to spend the children's inheritance by travelling as far and wide and as often as he can.

A new instalment in his *Exploring* series will soon be forthcoming from Extremis Publishing.

Also Available from Extremis Publishing

Exploring the NC500

Travelling Scotland's Route 66

By David M. Addison

Travelling anti-clockwise, David M. Addison seeks his kicks on Scotland's equivalent of Route 66. Otherwise known as NC500, the route takes you through five hundred miles of some of Scotland's most spectacular scenery. No wonder it has been voted as one of the world's five most scenic road journeys.

There are many ways of exploring the NC500. You can drive it, cycle it, motorbike it or even walk it, even if you are not one of The Proclaimers! And there are as many activities, places of interest and sights to be seen along the way as there are miles.

This is a personal account of the author's exploration of the NC500 as well as some detours from it, such as to the Black Isle, Strathpeffer and Dingwall. Whatever your reason or reasons for exploring the NC500 may be, you should read this book before you go, or take it with you as a *vade mecum*. It will enhance your appreciation of the NC500 as you learn about the history behind the turbulent past of the many castles; hear folk tales, myths and legends connected with the area; become acquainted with the ancient peoples who once lived in this timeless landscape, and read about the lives of more recent heroes such as the good Hugh Miller who met a tragic end and villains such as the notorious Duke of Sutherland, who died in his bed (and may not be quite as bad as he is painted). There are a good number of other characters too of whom you may have never heard: some colourful, some eccentric, some *very* eccentric.

You may not necessarily wish to follow in the author's footsteps in all that he did, but if you read this book you will certainly see the landscape through more informed eyes as you do whatever you want to do *en route* NC500.

Sit in your car and enjoy the scenery for its own sake (and remember you get a different perspective from a different direction, so you may want to come back and do it again to get an alternative point of view!), or get out and explore it at closer quarters – the choice is yours, but this book will complement your experience, whatever you decide.

Also Available from Extremis Publishing

Exploring the SWC300

A Cultural and Historical Companion to the South-West Coastal 300 Route

By David M. Addison

The SWC300 Route has been described as Scotland's Secret Corner – with some justification.

This book seeks to shed a light on the history and culture of this largely ignored part of Scotland. By delving into the colourful events that happened here in the past, the intention is to enhance and enrich your exploration of this land of contrasts as you travel through its rolling hills and along its spectacularly scenic coastline.

The Neolithic settlers, the first Christians, the medieval warlords and the reivers – all played a part in shaping this war-torn land. Sharing a common border with the Auld Enemy – the English – it was badly affected during the Wars of Independence, just as it was during the Covenanting period: what came to be called the Killing

Time. Sad to say, there were more deaths from disasters down the mines, out at sea, in the air, and in what remains, to this day, the UK's worst-ever rail disaster.

Follow in the footsteps of those who left their mark here. It's a varied cast of characters: kings, commoners and Covenanters; saints and sinners; murderers and martyrs; monks and ministers; poets and pioneers; engineers and explorers; artists and architects; geniuses and gypsies; writers and witches – even troglodytes and cannibals.

There are ruined castles and tower houses; grand houses and gardens; abbeys and churches; standing stones and stone circles; museums and monuments; retired railway engines and planes from yesteryear.

There are legends; folktales; and tales of the supernatural – all part of the rich tapestry that forms part of the greater and enthralling story that will be revealed to you as you explore what has been a neglected part of Scotland for far too long.

It's hard to imagine there can be another part of Scotland that has so much to offer the tourist.

Also Available from Extremis Publishing

The Heart 200 Book

A Companion Guide to Scotland's Most Exciting Road Trip

By Thomas A. Christie and Julie Christie

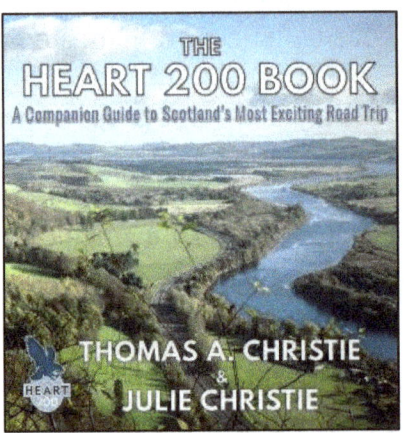

The Heart 200 route is a unique road trip around some of the most beautiful locations in Central Scotland. Two hundred miles running through Stirlingshire and Perthshire, Heart 200 takes its visitors on an epic adventure to suit every taste—whether you are an outdoors enthusiast, an aficionado of history, or simply looking to enjoy yourself in some of the most stunning natural surroundings in the world.

Written with the full approval and co-operation of the Heart 200 team, *The Heart 200 Book* is a guide to the very best that the route has to offer. You will discover the history and culture of this remarkable region, from antiquity to the modern day, with more than a few unexpected insights along the way. Over the millennia, this amazing land has made its mark on world history thanks to famous figures ranging from the ancient Celts and the Roman Empire to King Robert the Bruce and Mary Queen of Scots, by way of Bonnie Prince Charlie, Rob Roy MacGregor, Robert Burns, Sir Walter Scott, Queen Victoria and even The Beatles!

So whether you're travelling by foot, car, motorhome or bike, get ready for a journey like no other as the Heart 200 invites you to encounter standing stones and steamships, castles and chocolatiers, watersports and whisky distilleries... and surprising secrets aplenty! Illustrated with full-colour photography and complete with Internet hyperlinks to accompany the attractions, *The Heart 200 Book* will introduce you to some of the most remarkable places in all of Scotland and encourage you to experience each and every one for yourself. It really will be a tour that you'll never forget.

For details of new and forthcoming books from Extremis Publishing, please visit our official website at:

www.extremispublishing.com

or follow us on social media at:

www.facebook.com/extremispublishing

www.linkedin.com/company/extremis-publishing-ltd-/

www.ingramcontent.com/pod-product-compliance
Lightning Source LLC
Chambersburg PA
CBHW072012070526
44583CB00015B/1442